Improve Your Social Skills

Secrets of the World's Social Butterflies to Help Make Friends, Overcome Social Anxiety, and Start Conversations With Anyone ... Even if you're an Introvert

Text Copyright ©

All rights reserved. No part of this guide may be reproduced in any form without permission in writing from the publisher except in the case of brief quotations embodied in critical articles or reviews.

Legal & Disclaimer

The information contained in this book and its contents is not designed to replace or take the place of any form of medical or professional advice; and is not meant to replace the need for independent medical, financial, legal or other professional advice or services, as may be required. The content and information in this book has been provided for educational and entertainment purposes only.

The content and information contained in this book has been compiled from sources deemed reliable, and it is accurate to the best of the Author's knowledge, information and belief. However, the Author cannot guarantee its accuracy and validity and cannot be held liable for any errors and/or omissions. Further, changes are periodically made to this book as and when needed. Where appropriate and/or necessary, you must consult a professional (including but not limited to your doctor, attorney, financial advisor or such other professional advisor) before using any of the suggested remedies, techniques, or information in this book.

Upon using the contents and information contained in this book, you agree to hold harmless the Author from and against any damages, costs, and expenses, including any legal fees potentially resulting from the application of any of the information provided by this book. This disclaimer applies to any loss, damages or injury caused by the use and application, whether directly or indirectly, of any advice or information presented, whether for breach of contract, tort, negligence, personal injury, criminal intent, or under any other cause of action.

You agree to accept all risks of using the information presented inside this book.

You agree that by continuing to read this book, where appropriate and/or necessary, you shall consult a professional (including but not limited to your doctor, attorney, or financial advisor or such other advisor as needed) before using any of the suggested remedies, techniques, or information in this book.

Table of Contents

Section 1: Overview 1

Introduction 3

PART I: Back to Basics 5

Chapter 1: Understanding Social Skills 6

    Benefits of a Developed Social Skill 7

    The Reason Behind the Need to Socialize 9

Chapter 2: Why do you Want to Become
a Social Butterfly? 11

    Be Who You Are 12

    Be Interesting 13

    Be Aware of the Other Person 14

Chapter 3: Why Socializing is Important 15

    The Reason Behind the Need to Socialize 16

    Why Social Skills are Important 17

Section 2: Back to Basics 21

Chapter 4: Setting Your Social Goal 22
Determining and Comprehending Your Goals 23
Designing Fixed Practice Goals 24

Chapter 5: Social Anxiety 29
Two Types of Fear 32

Chapter 6: Physical Fear Vs.
Emotional Fear and Shyness 34
Difference Between Social Anxiety and Shyness 36

Chapter 7: Why Manipulation is Wrong? 37
Manipulation is Everywhere 38
Difference Between Coercion and Persuasion 38
Managing Through Manipulation 39
Positive Manipulation for a Positive Change 40

Chapter 8: Manners Maketh the Man and Woman 41
Why is Good Manners Important? 42

Chapter 9: Getting Comfortable, Feeling Uncomfortable ...45
Comfort Signals Field Guide 47
Discomfort Signals Field Guide 49

Chapter 10: Empathy and Mentorship 52
Understanding Your Emotions 53
Understanding Others 55
Non-verbal Empathy 56

The Importance of Having a Good Mentor.................................58

Chapter 11: Ordinary People...59

    Functional Interactions...59

    Person-to-Person Connection..59

Section 3: How to Improve Your Social Skills 63

Chapter 12: Starting Off Slow 64

    Social Level 64

    Mental Level 64

    Emotional Level...65

    Spiritual Level..65

Chapter 13: One Mouth and Two Ears..................................67

    Why Do We Need to Listen? 68

    The Art of Active Listening 68

Chapter 14: Giving Compliments 72

    Steps to Giving Great Compliments 72

Chapter 15: Acquaintances to Friends 75

    Finding and Meeting People 75

Chapter 16: Body Language 79

Chapter 17: Tone of Voice..81

    The Significance of the Tone of Voice and Why You Should Develop It 81

How Can You Improve Your Tone of Voice?............................83

Chapter 18: Keeping With the Conversation 86

    Invitation and Inspiration..86

    Invitation and Inspiration..87

    Inspiration in Good Conversation....................................88

    Harmonizing Invitation and Inspiration..........................90

Chapter 19: 100 Questions 91

    Invitation: The Art of Good Questioning.......................91

    Good Questions..92

Chapter 20: The Group Game Begins 94

    Joining Group Conversation 94

    Joining a Group..97

Chapter 21: How to Successfully End a Conversation 98

    Tell the Other Person Directly 98

    Give Reasons 98

    Use Non-verbal Language 99

Section 4: Improving Your Skills Depending on the Situation 101

Chapter 22: Dating 102

    Defining Healthy Relationships.....................................102

    Starting a Romantic Relationship 104

Chapter 23: Boundaries..106

How to Establish Healthy Personal Boundaries 106

Spot Signs of Unhealthy Boundaries 107

Chapter 24: Asperger's and Autism 109

Rote Memorization Issues 109

Learning by Understanding the Reasons Behind a Situation 110

Practical Applications 111

Chapter 25: Dealing With Children 113

Chapter 26: Dealing With Conflicts 117

Different Ways People Respond to Conflict 118

Emotions, Stress, and Conflict Resolution 119

Section 5: A Few Other Quickies 123

Chapter 27: Social Media 124

Effectively Responding to Negative Comments
on Social Media 124

Chapter 28: Random Encounters With Strangers 129

Give Out a Genuine Smile 130

Be Comfortable 131

Have an Open Body Language 131

Remember that Interaction is a Two-Way Communication .. 132

Be Yourself 132

Section 6: Mindset 133

Chapter 29: Using Habits to Change Your Mindset 134

Chapter 30: Why Journaling is so Important? 137

    Free Journaling 138

    Daily Recounting 139

    Creative Writing 139

Chapter 31: Improving Your Self-Esteem and Worth 140

    Get Away From Negative Thinking 141

    Take an Inventory 141

    Acknowledge Yourself 142

    Stop Comparing Yourself to Others 142

    Practice Self-Care 142

Chapter 32: How to Overcome Negative Thoughts 144

Chapter 33: The Importance of CBT 149

Conclusion 152

    Wrapping It Up 153

Book Description 157

Section 1

Overview

Introduction

Do you have this fear of speaking in public or even facing people in a social function?

Do you feel that you have inherent flaws in your character that through all these years you struggle hard interacting with other people? Well, it might not be something in your character that is the issue here but your lack of social skill.

Not everyone has an easy time going out to mingle with other people. Some are afraid they would embarrass themselves before the public and be a laughingstock. Others believe they don't belong anywhere else as they don't seem to fit to be seen with others. There are many reasons why these people are struggling hard in dealing with their social life because of something they believe in when they should not.

If you're one of these people, it's time that you lay aside this wrong belief. There's nothing wrong in you. You are the same as others who have their strengths, weaknesses, and potential. Everyone else has them and you're no different.

It's not because they are better than you. It's not because you aren't born to be smart that you need to hide and run away from them. They might not be as smart as you think or you could even be smarter than them. It's just that you don't believe in yourself. You don't have the confidence to show them what you've got so you stop believing in yourself.

It's time to get rid of those monsters that existed only on your thinking and had long enslaved your senses. It's time you unleash your full potentials if you don't want to continue suffering for the rest of your life.

There is much more to life than you had missed all the time because you allow these creepy monsters to lock you up in that dark, arid world of yours and be bound in your loneliness and sorrows.

It's time to reverse your MINDSET and get away from those bad thoughts that had long enslaved your senses. It's time to unleash your full potentials. You need no longer be afraid of facing anyone else and have this fear of being laughed at. You may have a few mistakes and some may laugh at you, but who cares? Everyone has their shares of faults and mistakes but what is important is how one deals with them. Situations are all temporary. They come and go. You don't need to lock up their memories inside that mind of yours so you can wallow in them amidst desperation.

This book will exactly help you get out of your nutshell to start believing in yourself. This will be your guide in developing your SOCIAL SKILLS – that essential skill you need to interact with people. It's time to learn how to use interaction to your benefits and this book will show you how to destroy those monsters that lurk inside your mind. Reading this book will unleash the real self that has long been locked up inside you and held hostage by those creepy creatures. Once free, only then can you experience how it is to live with your full potentials and how to use these potentials to make life easier and happier for you. Without those frightening thoughts that have long curtailed your real potentials and talents, success will be much easier to achieve. Dreams will no longer remain as dreams but will soon be a REALITY!

PART I

Back to Basics

CHAPTER 1:

Understanding Social Skills

Humans by nature are social creatures. From the day we are born until the day we die, we are and will be interacting with people – with our family, friends, acquaintances, co-workers, and even with a stranger we just meet on the street. We can't live in isolation. We need others to help and support us. Throughout our lives, we are interacting with other social creatures, who like us are living in a society where we need one another to survive. It is for this reason why we are born to socialize. We have this inherent social ability in us that needs to be developed just like the way when we were born as humans but had still had to undergo various processes of development before we can attain full maturity and achieve what we want in life.

Social skills are what we use to interact and communicate with others – verbally and nonverbally – through body language, speaking, gestures, and personal appearance. Being sociable creatures, we have developed many ways to communicate our thoughts, messages, and emotions to others.

The way we communicate is influenced by how we use both verbal language and non-verbal language. Verbal language involves our tone of voice, words we choose, and the volume of speech. Non-verbal communications refer to the more subtle messages we convey through our facial expressions, gestures, postures, body language, etc.

Human beings are sociable creatures and we have developed many ways to communicate our messages, thoughts, and feelings with others. Some people are better in interactions and communications than others which leads to a detailed investigation into the functions and nature of interpersonal interaction.

Developing social skills is about awareness of how we communicate with others – the messages we are relaying – and how different methods in communication can be improved to develop a more efficient and effective way of communicating.

Benefits of a Developed Social Skill

Having more developed and better communication skills has its distinct advantages. Here are some to point out.

Better Relationships With More People

Relating well with others leads to more relationships and connections which can result in friendships.

With a developed social skill, you tend to become more charismatic which is a desirable trait. People are generally drawn towards charismatic individuals as they prove to be interesting.

It is hard to advance in life without support from others, so one needs to develop a strong interpersonal relationship with others. Focusing on relationships can help you land a good job and expose you to a wider horizon. More and better relationships can also help you reduce the negative impact of stress while boosting your self-esteem and confidence.

Better Communications

Developing the ability to effectively relate to people enables you to work in a large group and naturally develop your communication skills. After all, social skills and communication skills work hand in hand. Being able to convey ideas and thoughts effectively could be one important skill you must develop in life.

The ability to communicate effectively with superiors, colleagues or co-workers is significant to one's success regardless of the industry you have chosen. Those working in the digital age must learn how to effectively convey and receive messages in person as well as via social media, phones, or emails.

Greater Efficiency

With good social skills, you can easily identify and avoid people you don't like to be with.

Some people dread social interactions because they hate spending time with people who don't share the same interests and viewpoints with them. It is a lot easier to be in social situations when you know there are people there whom you feel comfortable to share ideas with.

When you are in a social situation where you find yourself among those you don't enjoy being with, a good set of skills will help you politely get away from there and convey that you need to spend some time somewhere else.

Advancing Career Prospects

Worthwhile jobs have people as their major components and most lucrative positions require spending more time interacting with people. Seldom does it happen that an individual is required to stay isolated in their hub and still excel in their job? Corporate companies would often require employees and workers with a particular tactical skill set – the ability to synchronize well in a team and to be able to influence and motivate teammates to get things done.

Increased Overall Happiness

Understanding people and getting along with them help to open up many personal and career-related doors. Having the confidence to voice out your ideas and opinions and having the confidence to start a conversation in a work-related conference may open up better opportunities for you. A simple hello with the corresponding smile can win you more friends and connections and thereby give you more chance to enjoy life.

The Reason Behind the Need to Socialize

When people socialize with others, it helps the species to unite with one another. Because people require constant attention, people form small groups, which become tribes, communities or towns and cities depending on their number and capabilities. Even those with introverted behavior also need social interaction, even though they prefer to be left alone most of the time.

It is said that there is also power in numbers aside from the fact that people are more likely to reproduce and pass their genes when they socialize since it's easier to find a suitable partner if you have a member of the opposite sex in your group. There's also a possibility that the human civilizations that didn't find socializing a necessity didn't also pass their genes.

According to a physiological standpoint, social isolation is associated with death in older adults, hence being considered not a healthy practice. It is said that this situation leads to increased HPA activation and tonic sympathetic tonus, decreased immunity and inflammatory control, gene expression regulating the response of glucocorticoids as well as sleep salubrity. Altogether, these lead to higher chances of mortality and morbidity in older adults.

Looking at the neurological or psychological standpoint, solitary confinement of prison mates is associated with higher rates of mental illness and suicide cases inside the prison in addition to the reduced cerebral cortex, the part of the brain responsible for language production and perception.

There are cases that the prisoners were put in solitary confinement because of their psychological issues, though evidence also suggests that social isolation also leads to their decreased feelings of self-worth, depression, and loss of self-esteem.

CHAPTER 2:

Why do you Want to Become a Social Butterfly?

Socializing can be rather awkward especially for an introvert – meeting people, dating, mingling with new connections and attending social gatherings. There is more to add to the list. Regardless of the event, the situation can still be uncomfortable.

On the other hand, there are unique species of people who can be very intriguing to watch. They can walk in a room and all heads would automatically turn in their direction. They can effortlessly attract people and thrive in the center of attraction. They are SOCIAL BUTTERFLIES.

Social butterflies live such an active social life that so many of us would envy as they make life look so easy. Ever dream of becoming a social butterfly? Have you ever put yourself down because you're nothing close to it? Do you want to get over the struggle of socializing and develop a social skill?

We are expected to connect throughout our life despite our unwillingness to engage, background, or perspective in life. This can be difficult especially when you don't have the skill to socialize. Besides the basic niceties of being polite and good ethics we have learned at home and in school, there is more to learn to develop your social skills.

Social butterflies are those who know just how to make the party alive. The exactly knows how to liven up a room, make connections, and live every person in that room in a lighter state than when they found them. Social butterflies are easy to connect with as they possess and showcase an enjoyment with interacting. They can make you feel valued and easily create a sense of ease with the exchange of communication.

Some people do have a natural gift for interacting with ease and style and some don't. And if you think that you are either born with this special gift or not, then you better think otherwise for this skill can be acquired with practice and you must be willing to step out of your comfort zone.

Here are some tips on how to develop your social wings and communicate with ease as a social butterfly.

Be Who You Are

Some destructive socializing patterns sneak in more frequently than you may realize like people-pleasing, self-editing, and inauthentic expressions.

If you misjudge yourself or see yourself as someone incompetent in socializing, you may try to fix it by emulating someone you see better – usually a social butterfly. Doing it can only develop a forced, scripted, and inauthentic way of interacting that is neither fun nor productive. You must always remember that butterflies, like people, have their unique looks and specific way of flying. Copying someone would only make you a fake channel of communication that will only result in stale interactions.

If you aren't yourself, then you aren't emitting the radiance that can enlighten people you came in contact with. This will also leave you to feel depleted and dissatisfied regardless of how many people you have interacted with. You don't need to be like someone you aren't just to please people.

Being someone that you aren't will only make you lose more of your confidence and give you that feeling of guilt. If you think you are making yourself different from who you were before, you're probably right – only that you're creating the worst one than before!

It's always better to show the world the REAL YOU! People can always sense when you aren't who you are. Communicating with people comes from the inside and not from something that's outside of you. Remember that real talks come from relating heart to heart.

Be Interesting

When interacting, most people push it hard – trying to appear more successful, funny or smart. They fill up conversations with facts and stories about them and forcing people to believe them. In the end, it turned out to be a monologue instead of a dialogue – which is a two-way interaction.

As soon as you realized that you're doing this, STOP! Ask something instead to the one you're speaking. People love to be heard than to simply listen throughout what should be your interaction activity. You may want to be remembered for caring enough to take an interest in them rather than someone conceited.

When in a conversation with someone who is trying to make a push, acknowledge them for how they want to be seen. If they are pushing to appear as someone funny, laugh at their jokes. If they want to be seen as successful, compliment them on their successes. From there, drive to another topic and see if they follow you from there.

People who are pushing hard usually relax and allow the conversation to turn more natural once you have acknowledged them. If not, find ways to make a graceful exit as there is no need to stay in a conversation that does not allow you to interact.

Be Aware of the Other Person

Communication is a two-way street. So when there is a communication difficulty or breakdown which hampered the smooth delivery of communication, better ask where the other person is functioning from.

Most often, we blame ourselves for this and don't take the time to recognize that the person on the other end of the communication is bored, self-involved or not open to connecting, least interacting. If this is the case, there is no reason to blame yourself. Don't make yourself solely responsible for the outcome in the exchange of communication.

By harnessing your skills as a social butterfly, you can work on its advantage – both personally and professionally.

CHAPTER 3:

Why Socializing is Important

Socializing is how we learn to be cultured or behave in a way that is acceptable to society. It helps shape us even in ways we neither realize nor understand. This includes both formal and informal ways of learning which occur through interacting with other people in society.

From the time of your birth, you start learning those values and norms of your culture - the norms that define how people interact with each other. We learn how to walk, talk, eat and behave differently in different places and occasions through socialization.

The Reason Behind the Need to Socialize

When people socialize with others, it helps the whole humanity to unite with one another. Because people require constant attention, people form small groups, which become tribes, communities or towns and cities depending on their number and capabilities. Even those with introverted behavior also need social interaction, even though they prefer to be left alone most of the time. It is said that there is also power in numbers aside from the fact that people are more likely to reproduce and pass their genes when they socialize since it's easier to find a suitable partner if you have a member of the opposite sex in your group. There's also a possibility that the human civilizations that didn't find socializing a necessity didn't also pass their genes.

According to a physiological standpoint, social isolation is associated with death in older adults, hence being considered not a healthy practice. It is said that this situation leads to increased HPA activation and tonic sympathetic tonus, decreased immunity and inflammatory control, gene expression regulating the response of glucocorticoids as well as sleep in salubrity. Altogether, these lead to higher chances of mortality and morbidity in older adults.

Looking at the neurological or psychological standpoint, solitary confinement of prison mates is associated with higher rates of mental illness and suicide cases inside the prison in addition to the reduced cerebral cortex – the part of the brain responsible for language production and perception.

There are cases that the prisoners were put in solitary confinement because of their psychological issues, though evidence also suggests that social isolation also leads to their decreased feelings of self-worth, depression, and loss of self-esteem.

Why Social Skills are Important

Social skills impact our everyday actions. From the moment we greet someone with a simple "hello" to forging relationships with those around you, we are interacting with fellow human beings. By learning face-to-face interaction, we are provided with many benefits. Human beings are animals and thus need the skills to interact effectively within the society

Social Skills are Critical

Learning face-to-face social skills provides several benefits. Human beings are social animals and the skill to interact within society is required to function effectively.

Children today have many opportunities to socialize. Nowadays, they are spending hours on social media via their digital devices – handset, tablets, and PC. Through the internet, they were allowed to communicate and interact with as many people as they can. Having a social network of friends provides a support network – helping each other in providing solutions to some issues, facing a challenge, or dealing with difficult situations.

Having positive social skills increases levels of understanding and empathy towards each other and positive social interaction promotes understanding of other viewpoints.

When you belong to a social group like communities, it can help eliminate feelings of isolation while promoting improved overall social, mental, and emotional well-being. People who are accepted in a group tend to be more satisfied and happier in general.

Social skills can make or break a relationship or a pleasant conversation. It can also make or break a business negotiation. You may think that the ability to hold a conversation, actively listen, and be engaging is something not necessary and everyone is doing that every moment. Nonetheless, these are not just simply skills, but an important commodity in any business condition.

Inside the technology sector, it is often acceptable for developers and engineers to have poor social skills but these are stereotypes. When one has a strong presence and the ability to connect with others in a network, it is considered an invaluable resource.

Social Skills Are the Foundation of Healthy Relationships

Social skills are significant to a healthy relationship either with your loved one, family, friends, co-workers, and colleagues. With the right social skills, it would be easy for you to integrate into any groups or communities, socialize, and form connections. You can easily expand your audience or market base when marketing your brand and meet potential partners in life or business. It allows you to connect with people on levels that are significant in life for you to develop a more in-depth partnership with them. To be able to relate effectively with people, you need a reliable communication channel that you can use to convey your message properly and is essential to every message you want to communicate.

When communicating with people face-to-face or by phone calls or text messaging, your communication channel is your social skills. Those people who have poor social skills find it difficult to interact with others – especially with strangers, making it hard for them to meet new people and expand their network.

Social Skills Allow You to Initiate Contacts

Social Skills are very useful in approaching potential business partners, making friends, or merely starting a conversation with someone that caught your interest. When you know how to effectively initiate connection so that others will feel comfortable interacting with you, you will be meeting more new acquaintances and thus quickly build a bigger network. The more people you have in your network, the quicker it will be to add more and expand your network of social acquaintances.

Science proves through research studies that more than 70% of your messages conveyed does not come from words you relayed but from emotions imparted. What is important to people is not what they hear but how they feel when they hear them. If they feel good while having interaction with you, they are sure to appreciate things you've said and will look forward to another interaction with you soon. On the contrary, if they feel dismayed with the conversation they have with you, they would desire to see you see again and do everything in their power to avoid meeting you. When this happens, it just means one thing – you have poor social skills and you fail to relate to their emotions.

Social Skills Allow You to Understand Others Effectively

When you have good social skills, you can relate to other people effectively. You can understand what they need and know exactly how to deliver them. Social skills come with the ability to sense people – their wants, desires, and intentions. This ability will enhance your adaptability to people you are connecting with which is extremely important in any form of interaction.

Ultimately, having social skills develops in you a strong charismatic personality that can influence people. It would be easy for you to persuade them to believe in your ideas or stand on issues without much effort on your part. This will, of course, provide you with many opportunities that will help improve your life and ultimately attain success.

Social Skills Strengthen Your Credibility

Having the ability to communicate effectively comes along with communicating through the heart. As this helps you connect with people via their heart and mind, it strengthens your credibility. When you can explain well your ideas or stand on certain issues, people can instantly relate to you and believe you. This means, they find you more credible – which an essential component of integrity. People are easily influenced by those who have integrity and actions that strongly support their credibility.

Although being an introvert may have its benefit but being sociable both in person and on social media platforms can quickly expand your network of friends and acquaintances.

Section 2

Back to Basics

CHAPTER 4:

Setting Your Social Goal

Goals are utilized in two ways. The first approach is when you begin to plan and pen them down. This helps you map out the ideas, making them clearer and easier to deal with. The second approach is when you implement these ideas and strategies for a particular amount of time. Everyone can benefit in the first; while the second one is more suitable if you've already achieved a specific mindset and motivation.

Determining and Comprehending Your Goals

Anyone who wants to have a progress in their social situation has goals. Nevertheless, that doesn't mean that they have given enough thought or allotted much time about those thoughts. When you determine your goals, what you must do first is to take indefinite statements in your mind such as:

- I am sad and lonely…
- I'm unsatisfied with all of these…
- I want to be visible…
- I look lame and unfashionable…

Jot them down in a piece of paper. The purpose of this is to help you determine what your overall social are. You may want to expand your circle of friends, be more confident, and look more fashionable. It's okay if you still don't have specific goals at this point.

Next, you may want to devise up some mid-sized goals by determining the obstacles that may prevent you from achieving your overall goal. At first, you may easily figure this out, but it's fairly common to commit mistakes or have miscalculations. This just means that you still have room for improvement. You must educate yourself more. For instance, you're having difficulty with fashion, but if you read more fashion magazines you will learn which colors and clothes can enhance your appearance.

Another method you can use is visualization. Imagine that you're achieving your broader goal as you recall the strategies you implemented to draw closer to your goals. Which areas are still having doubts, negative thoughts, fears, or self-critical thoughts? What instances do you still feel unhappy or disheartened? Let's say, when you think about how you still want to be more confident, you may suddenly start feeling stressed that you're not confident enough. What's the problem? Is this something that you must do?

For this, you can create a list of sub-goals to address your dilemma and boost your confidence:
- I will try to develop my personality more.
- I will try to interact more with people regardless of race, social standing, or sexual orientation.
- I will try to achieve a fit body; ergo, a fit mind.
- I will groom myself to enhance my image.

You can even break down those mid-sized goals into more detailed ones. These may be specific tasks you can do. For instance:
- I will take a Personality Development course.
- I will interact with different people and travel abroad to learn more about different societies.
- I will exercise daily to achieve a fit body and healthy inner well-being.
- I will try to learn how to dress fashionably and smartly to enhance my image.

You may also want to try things that may not be directly tied with your larger objectives. For example, you may want to try a join a cause and extend your blessing to other people to develop your sense of belongingness to the society. This, in a way, also boosts your confidence and self-worth.

Don't worry or feel discouraged if what you've come up with isn't perfect or complete. You can always make adjustments as you learn more.

Designing Fixed Practice Goals

Everyone can profit from mapping out their goals. Nonetheless, individuals will differ in how they implement those goals. One possibility is to allocate a certain period to actively work on your goals. Let's say, you may decide to devote a couple of weeks to a couple of months in taking a Personality Development course. Making your goals SMART (specific, measurable, achievable, realistic, and timely) can help you structure your goals effectively.

On the other hand, it's still okay to pursue your goals more casually. Some people tend to perform more effectively that way. They want to do things more spontaneously, but don't get them wrong—they certainly know what issues they want to work on. Not everyone has a huge sense of urgency about changing and that's okay. While some people believe that clear goals get them focused and motivated, others feel pressured by them. Below are some common suggestions for setting quality practice goals:

Make Goals That Are Achievable in About Two to Six Months

You don't' want your goal to be something achievable in just a short while. That's something you can consider as a short-term objective rather than a bigger goal. Meanwhile, you don't want to aim for something that would take a few years to fulfill. For instance, if you're currently having low self-confidence, you wouldn't want to set a goal that goes like, "I will study modeling and undergo a 'glow-up' and everybody will look up to me. By then, I will be confident enough to face all people no matter what the situation is." Setting a medium-term goal like taking a Personality Development course and revamping your wardrobe can be a good starting point.

Set an Exciting but Realistic Goals

Your goals should be challenging and attainable at the same time. If they're too easy, you'll just achieve them quickly and you'll have to come up with a harder one to set up again. On the other hand, developing a goal enough to make you break a sweat will make you feel enthusiastic and motivated about it for a while. Just make sure that the goal is achievable within your reserved timeframe.

Don't Focus on Many Goals at Once

Don't try to face your social problems head-on all at once. You may feel impatient to get your life in order as soon as possible. However, these things take time and shouldn't be expedited. You need a particular amount of willpower and courage to appropriately handle challenging goals, and if you've got too much of it, you can't concentrate on achieving them. But this is not to say that you can't work on other goals every now and then. What you need is to work on manageable goals. Remember, keep it real!

Make Concrete and Measurable Goals

To put it in simple terms, what you need is to put your goals, as well as the sub-tasks required of it, into action. This is the crucial part since it allows you to figure out to produce specific tasks to practice and monitor your progress. Let's give you a few examples:

Mid-sized Goals

- Speaking confidently- enroll in a speech class
- Overcoming fear of social events- by the end of three months, I should be able to attend a party and stay for at least one or two hours.
- Feeling less shy or awkward with new people- measure the level of your anxiety or shyness (scale from 1 to 10) when interacting with new people. Monitor and record how you felt during such times within three months. Write down how

you felt during these interactions and make efforts to change average rating down from an 8 to a 4.

Sub-Goals

- Speaking confidently, performing visualization exercises and speaking in front of the mirror every morning or night
- Overcoming fear of social events- practice relaxation techniques 10 to 15 minutes a day
- Feeling less shy or awkward with new people- after a particular social interaction, reflect on your thoughts and feelings that came up during and after the event. Manage the negative ones.

As you may have noticed, social goals aren't easily adapted to be objective and measurable compared to other goals such as losing weight or learning how to cook. One of the reasons for this is that social skills are subjective. Even if you can measure some aspects of it, it still doesn't capture the whole story.

Therefore, you don't have to worry over things whether you need to begin making two to three friends within two weeks or so. Remember, these are people who may have different reactions, priorities, set of activities, and goals. You possibly couldn't have too much influence with people whom you just met. These factors make it hard for you to achieve goals. Nevertheless, you don't have to easily dismiss a goal simply because you weren't able to maintain a fifteen-minute talk with a person! The beauty of this is that you can adjust your target that provides you a rough estimate of where you want to be.

It's Fine to Modify a Goal

Starting a goal doesn't mean that you're already off to a steady direction. Of course, there would be bumps or miscalculations along the way—those are natural. At times, you need to adjust the difficulty of a level or you'll realize that you don't need a certain task to accomplish your goal. You can always modify your steps.

Always start with little steps instead of charging full ahead. Goals like wanting to *be the most popular man on earth* or the *most admired personality in the world* are but ambiguous fantasy goals. While these thoughts can be motivating or exciting, they're also unhealthy.

Timid and shy people tend to think that being the Most Popular Guy or Gal catapults them into the person they want to be. Goals like this are highly disadvantageous. They can put too much pressure on people. Furthermore, they make people feel that unless things work smoothly, they're failures. Rather than working for something utterly amazing, try to start with a realistic and modest goal.

CHAPTER 5:

Social Anxiety

Social anxiety is the fear of being judged or laughed at - of saying or doing the wrong things in a social situation. This fear of facing social situations could have stemmed from an experience or experiences which left them a high level of strain on their emotions. Probably they have experienced great humiliation in the past or were judged wrongly for anything they have done or said. Sometimes it could even involve wearing the wrong clothes or being associated with someone despised by whoever caused them great humiliation.

Most often, people with social anxiety also want to participate and interact to have lasting and meaningful relationships with others, but their fear of being humiliated plus those anxious thoughts inhibit their ability for interaction.

They also don't like this feeling and tend to mentally berate themselves every time they feel it happening. Having social anxiety could also mean the presence of other social disorders including alcohol or drug dependence, depression, and eating disorders.

Expecting to be rejected or focusing too much on an intense reaction will only lead to self-fulfilling something you greatly fear.

The anxious feeling we have when we are facing new or stressful situations is triggered by our "fight or flight response". This is an automatic reaction of our brain once we are facing danger or what we presume to be dangerous.

When you decide to stand your ground to face the danger that lurks before you, that's your "fight response" and the "flight response" is when you want to remove yourself from what you feel is an immediate danger.

For normal people, these two responses are programmed properly and are not activated in situations when there is no real danger such as when you go on a blind date or enroll in a new school. However, there are cases when the fight or flight mode is set off in the same situations.

You have no control over these feelings. You need to work hard to rewire your brain to recognize anxious signals and refrain it from having an automatic fear response as your mind reflexes react adversely when you are confronted with uncomfortable social situations.

To be able to overcome what inhibits you, you must be aware of the triggers that lead you to these reactions and the work to reduce the negativity associated with it.

Although your friends will tell you not to worry or get anxious over things, they are not experiencing things as you do. They are not aware of how difficult it is for you to simply attend a social event or gathering without this feeling of wanting to turn around and walk away. They don't know that simply being there requires you to gather all the courage available just to face the fear that instantly puts you on the fight or flight mode.

In some cases, an imbalance in chemicals may occur in the brain. Serotonin which is a chemical in the brain is responsible for managing and regulating moods and emotional reactions. In people suffering from social anxiety, the production of serotonin is found to be lowered or dampened. This causes the irrational sense associated with nervousness and fear.

The underproduction of the brain chemical may be a physiological matter; you may use psychological effort to boost the production with some practice. You may find medications to treat social anxiety but their effects are but temporary and sometimes, it won't even work in your condition. Sometimes, its side effects may also be worse than the ailment itself. It is for such reason that some people don't want to take drug medication for treatment. A physiological reaction can be an underlying cause of your shyness or social anxiety. However, drug medication is not the sole treatment for social anxiety or shyness you are experiencing. There are also natural and sustainable methods to manage them.

Nevertheless, let us first study the two types of fear and their differences.

Two Types of Fear

When you are facing a burglar who managed to enter your home in the middle of the night, your body is alerting you of the great danger before you. You can feel the adrenaline rush as your heart beats rapidly as your head starts screaming of DANGER!

In a situation like this, your reflex system is turned ON and every nerve in your body is alerting every muscle to protect you. All senses are heightened and work together to protect you. Your whole body is focused on making one of these two choices: fight or flight. This is REAL FEAR.

However, here is another kind of fear that exists only in your thinking. Everything is in your head. You imagine the danger and threat when in reality, it can't hurt you. It's you who create the fear and it can harm you only because you allow it.

An example of this imagined fear is when you are about to speak before a large audience. You visualize people laughing at you while you stammer in your speech. Others could even be shouting at you and telling you to get lost. This sends you into a panic attack and this thing is happening only in your brain but it can send your body into paralysis. We call this SOCIAL ANXIETY.

See the difference between the two kinds of FEAR?

The Real Fear is your body's way of alerting you about the danger before you while Physical Fear is what we call social anxiety which is being activated by your brain in response to your fear.

Social anxiety can only hurt you if you succumb to it. However, it affects the mental and emotional areas which make it more difficult to handle than the real fear.

Now, let's get back to what happens in your mind when facing a situation that normally faces you feel shy or frightened.

- Does the thought of interacting with people you haven't met before frightened you?

- Do you feel awkward being in a group that you tend to become quiet?
- Do you feel sweat suddenly streaming down your forehead and palms when someone approaches you?
- Do you find it hard to hold a conversation with someone?

What is the first thought that usually sprung up when you feel the fear of facing people?

Your past experiences are what usually determine your thoughts in the present moment. So if you feel anxious facing people, it could be that you have experienced being humiliated or bullied in your childhood. Most of the time, it's the parents or teachers who usually create a big impact on children.

To start, be aware of your initial thoughts once you experience the symptoms of social anxiety and from, work until you are reminded of what triggered them in the first place.

Social anxiety and shyness may have some physical side effects such as sweaty palms and racing thoughts. You may also find it difficult to formulate words and connect with your voice. In short, you have this tendency to be tongue-tied. Your series of negative thoughts will be compounded by such negative experiences leading to more anxiety or panic attacks.

There is always a cause for social anxiety. It is always the thought that comes before it. Although thoughts are not initially positive nor negative, the emotion brought about by those thoughts is what designates it to be positive or negative. This emotion is a conditioned reaction from previous experiences that can either be your own experience or those of people close to you.

Once your mind recognizes the negative emotion linked to that certain thought in a social situation, it starts the cycle of negative thoughts.

CHAPTER 6:

Physical Fear Vs. Emotional Fear and Shyness

If you read the previous chapters, you should be able to get a good idea of the difference between Physical Fear (Real Fear) and Emotional Fear (Social Anxiety) so concentrate more on social anxiety versus shyness.

Shyness and social anxiety both stemmed from fear – the fear of being judged, the fear of being seen as a misfit in any situation, or the fear of saying something wrong which can lead to criticisms. However, shyness and social anxiety come from different areas of the mind.

While shyness is the feeling of being awkward and tense around others, social anxiety is much deeper than shyness as it is the fear of being judged and criticized negatively by others.

For people suffering from social anxiety, they fear social situations that they entirely avoid them. In cases where they can't avoid being in one of these situations, they suffer through them in extreme fear – putting a high level of emotional strain on themselves.

They have this great fear of being humiliated or criticized for what they may say or do. They also expect to go through judgment because of what they wear.

Individuals suffering from social anxiety are likewise shy, but not all do. Others have social anxiety but not shy. Studies prove that approximately 50% of those with social anxiety are also shy.

Most often, those with social anxiety desire to interact with others and form lasting friendships or relationships but their fear of being humiliated or criticized is what inhibits them from establishing a connection or attention to social events. They also hate themselves for going through such negative emotions and continually berate themselves when experiencing them. Living with social anxiety can also mean mental disorders like alcohol and drug dependence, depression, and eating disorders.

On the other hand, shyness is considered a character trait and shy people don't think it's a bad one. Although they may experience anxiety and may worry about saying the wrong words and doing the wrong things, they can maintain a good mood and not suffer from negative and irrational thoughts.

Once shy people get familiar with their surroundings, they easily get past their social concerns. While shyness and social anxiety may not be the same, but there's a tendency for shyness to evolve into social anxiety under certain conditions.

Allowing your shyness to keep you from exploring new things or letting your focus distracted especially by negative thinking, as well as withdrawing from your peers will nurture the condition leading to social anxiety. Moreover, when you are having unrealistic expectations or drawing conclusions that are quite irrational about any upcoming social events could eventually exacerbate your shyness and turn it into full-pledge social anxiety.

Difference Between Social Anxiety and Shyness

Someone shy will experience a fast beating of the heart and will feel more conscious of their physical appearance. On the other hand, the one experiencing social anxiety experience sweating and a notable increase in heart, the thought of being not good enough and the fear of anticipating that everything they say or do will garner criticisms and judgment.

After a time of being exposed in a social situation, someone who is shy will start to adjust with the surrounding that this feeling of shyness lessens until it will eventually disappear. But the one suffering from social anxiety will not get relief from its symptoms unless they separate themselves from the social situation.

Someone shy may come from a family where one or two people may have shyness and nervousness. The one with social anxiety exists with the memory of ever-exaggerated rejection and extreme social awkwardness.

Shyness has been a part of one's personality while social anxiety can build from past experiences.

CHAPTER 7:

Why Manipulation is Wrong?

Nobody wants to get manipulated in any way. Whether it is our personal or professional life, manipulation is nonetheless considered a bad thing to do.

Most people associate manipulation with negative connotations, especially when it comes to people who want us to do things we don't want to do. However, does anyone think about the potential of manipulation to promote positive change? Believe it or not, manipulation can be a good thing, surprising as it may sound.

Manipulation is Everywhere

Whether people realize it or not, both their personal and professional lives are already being manipulated in more ways than one. This kind of "power" is already being harnessed and embraced by businesses and marketers to make us buy their goods and live our lives in a way they think of.

- Eat more vegetables and lessen cholesterol intake.
- Buy this shoe brand. Buy this dress brand.
- Vote for this politician.
- Quit smoking since it is bad for your health.
- Drink moderately.

Seeing the examples above, we can say that, even though it's somewhat manipulative, asking people to quit smoking is a good thing. Hence, we can say that this is a kind of positive manipulation.

Difference Between Coercion and Persuasion

By definition, manipulation means to control someone, something or a situation in a skillful manner. Taking a look at this, manipulation doesn't have any negative connotations. However, keep in mind that the use of this so-called influence could become positive or negative, depending on whether the deed involves coercion or persuasion.

For managers and employers, it is essential to understand and determine the difference between the two. Coercion simply means getting people to do what they don't want to do. Persuasion, on the other hand, means getting people to do what they want to do in the first place. Effective managers and employers make sure that they are aware of the difference between these two for them not to get confused. Needless to say, coercion is a form of harassment or bullying when used inside a workplace while persuasion in a workplace appears in the form of encouragement or motivation.

Managing Through Manipulation

A good manager makes sure that his team is always motivated while diligently doing their work. This is an essential part of professional development especially for employees that benefit both the individuals themselves as well as the organization. Positively manipulating staff is an effective management tool. Positive forms of manipulation motivate employees to help improve their overall performance as well as allow their teams to achieve organizational goals as soon as possible.

According to Jonathon Fields, coercion and persuasion can be differentiated by the three things which are stated below:

- The intention behind the wish or desire to manipulate the person.
- The end benefits or impact on the manipulated person.
- The transparency and truthfulness behind the manipulation process.

Whenever you look for a behavioral change from a new employee or team member, as a manager or employer, you should always reflect or ask yourself about the reasons for wanting to manipulate or influence that person's behavior. Looking at this will let you know whether your actions benefit the person or not. It's also very important to focus on your aim while maintaining your values to influence your staff positively.

Positive Manipulation for a Positive Change

Good kinds of manipulation are usually utilized by non-profit organizations as well as ethical companies to persuade people to take the necessary action by helping the needy and promoting positive change to those around them.

In her article, "Manipulating People, but in a Good Way," Margaret Kelsey, the writer questioned whether this is the right way to use such power. According to her, individuals have this power that could change people's behavior. However, she wants to know whether manipulation by using a psychological approach to raise funds or attract sponsors is a positive thing or even the right thing to do.

In conclusion, manipulation can be a good or bad thing, depending on the person's motive and intention behind the manipulation. However, also keep in mind that, along the way, those motives and intentions are subject to change. After all, nothing is written in stone.

CHAPTER 8:

Manners Maketh the Man and Woman

Manners define an individual while etiquette is what makes him socially acceptable.

Manners define an individual while etiquette is what makes him socially acceptable. These two virtues can help a man or a woman gains respect from other people. It also creates a good and lasting impression of who they are.

Manners are what you carry with you every day to make a good impression on others and to feel good about yourself. Regardless of where you are - at home, work, or with friends - practicing good manners is important.

Manners give you a chance to create a good impression on others and to feel good about oneself. Regardless of where you are, whether at home, at work, with friends or family, practicing good manners is very important.

Good manners are more than greeting your teachers or giving way to elders and disabled. It is considering how others may feel. It embraces empathy and compassion.

By practicing good manner, you are initiating a standard of good behavior for others to follow as you encourage them to treat you with similar respect.

Every individual and culture have different concepts and views of what good behavior is. So here we are going to review some of the basic and common rules of good behavior in our society. As rules may differ depending on a certain situation, there is one universal rule – the Golden Rule of good manners that is easy to follow.

"Do to others what you want others to do to you."

While practicing good manners, you are showing people around you that you are respectful and considerate of their feelings, thus setting yourself a good example for others to follow.

Manners and etiquette touch every aspect of our lives. From the time we were born, they have been ingrained in our minds. Manners represent one's inner self while etiquette is how one portrays himself in public.

Common courtesies like being polite to your elders and saying please and thank you are just some of the basic manners that one must be able to exercise early in life.

Why is Good Manners Important?

Good Manner Help Your Gain Respect from Others

The way you conduct yourself mirrors your inner personality. The way you smile and how you greet others are the first things people will notice in you and thus create the first impression of you. Manners define your character and influence your attitude. People see who you are through the way you treat others regardless of their status in life. As the golden rule says, "Treat others just like the way you want to be treated." So when you treat others with respect, expect to receive respect in return.

Good Manners Add Charm to Your Personality

When you are well mannered, it enhances your personality. It added extra charm which can be an added advantage to your social skills. Note that manners are acquired and adapted and go a long way. If you have high regard for your parents, your children will see it and will imitate you. Good manners can be contagious in a way that when people around you constantly observed your good manners, before they notice it, they are soon following your ways.

Good Manners Make Relationships Smoother

Manners teach you to be considerate of the feelings and emotions of others just as it teaches you to be polite. So even when some people behave badly in front of you, your good manners will stop you from giving out negative responses. While you gain better control over yourself and your emotions, you are teaching other people how to interact properly and treat people with respect. These manners will govern the way to act and respond to situations.

People think highly of good-mannered individuals that when you are identified as good-mannered, building relationships will be easier for you.

Good Manners Help Increase Your Confidence

Practicing good manners helps you gain more confidence and makes you more aware of your surroundings. They are like magnets that draw people towards you. Thus being sympathetic to others and not make fun of their deformities will determine your attitude while confidence will determine your perception of things and your responses to situations. The practice of good manners is a good stepping stone if you want to reach success in life.

Good Manners Keep You Motivated and Happy

Many virtues are universally accepted. When you are generous and kind to others as well as maintaining a peaceful, calm, and compose stature even in the worst times helps earn respect from others. These are essentials to a happy life and being highly respected constantly keeps you motivated.

Good Manners Impart Strength to Take Failure

It's not easy to take failures but good manners teach you to accept them. In life, we are constantly forced to face challenges to test our patience, but with good manners, you develop that positive outlook in life to help you maintain your composure and turn the tide in your favor.

CHAPTER 9:

Getting Comfortable, Feeling Uncomfortable

B ody language is a kind of gesture and action that helps people understand each other. If you meet a friend and their body language displays terror or sadness, it's only natural for you to ask them what's going on. And if you tell a story and your friends show interest through their body language, it will persuade you to keep talking. Needless to say, it's very useful and yet, it's also very complex.

Body language is complex in a way that there are lots, probably hundreds of different body languages. Unless you put a considerable amount of effort, there is no way for you to learn them all. However, there are only two body language signals for you to learn, that is, Comfort and Discomfort.

Comfort signals tell you if the person you're with is feeling good. People send off comforting signals if they like the person they are with or if they enjoy their talk or activity.

Discomfort signals, on the other hand, are being sent by people if they're uncomfortable with their conversation or activity with the person they're with. They don't show enjoyment or happiness in whatever they are doing.

Responses to Comfort and Discomfort

Whether you like it or not, comfort and discomfort signals are being sent by people depending on the situation they are in. Knowing this simple fact will not just give you an advantage; it will also give you hints or clues about your partner's feelings, hence giving you the time to think of doing the necessary action.

You can compare these signals to green and red traffic lights. If your partner gives off a green or comfort signal whenever you do something, you can continue your actions as you wish. In other words, you can just enjoy and relax while savoring the moment. However, if your partner gives off a red or discomfort signal, you might as well stop whatever you are doing and, in some cases, be ready for an apology. Also, keep in mind that a green signal could turn into a red one and vice versa depending on the situation.

If you happen to get a red light from your conversation partner, it is your responsibility to start a conversation in a way that will make them comfortable. It's much better if you can easily identify the things or matters that make them feel uncomfortable and prevent those from ruining your conversation. In other words, observe their body language. If they feel comfortable, you can relax. Otherwise, pause for a while, find out what's wrong and try to fix it.

Practicing Comfort and Discomfort Signals

Practicing these two signals is simple and easy if you have common sense. Knowing to give out a quick and precise answer whenever your partner asks questions is comforting while lengthy and misleading answers usually cause discomfort. Your partner may not have the courage or guts to say that they're bored to your face. In such cases, checking out their body language is necessary. Once done, observe their body language for positive changes.

People display comfort and discomfort through body language at all times so you must learn how to identify and understand those. Doing this will make your interaction with others much easier. You need to be able to notice the differences between comfort and discomfort signals as well as looking at the context of the conversation to determine what's wrong.

Comfort Signals Field Guide

Whenever you talk with someone, comfort signals are necessary. If your partner is comfortable, it means that you can relax and lengthen your conversation.

People show comfort in various ways, the most important ones are mentioned below. Your goal is to identify the signal patterns to those. If the person you are talking to is comfortable, they will send multiple comfort signals.

Listed below are the comfort signals that are common and easy to identify. Keep in mind, however, that those signals aren't one hundred percent reliable to say that the person you're talking to is comfortable.

Leaning or Moving Closer to Face You

When someone is comfortable or interested in whatever you say, they usually want to remove or lessen the distance between the two of you. You can think of this as their move for piquing their interest.

Removing such distance usually appears in various forms. Sometimes they will turn to face you, scoot closer or, if you know each other long enough, lean towards you. Sometimes they will even remove obstructions along the way, like bags or throw pillows on the sofa between the two of you.

The feet are a somewhat reliable indicator when someone turns to face you. If the person you're talking to does this, it means that they are comfortable.

Head Resting on a Hand/Tilted Head

If a person rests his head on one hand, it means that he's paying attention to what you are saying. The tilted head, on the other hand, means that he is curious about the topic. If they are comfortable, you will even see them lean forward while resting their elbows on the table or desk.

Physical Touch

A significant indicator of one's comfort, physical touch is done by people whenever they are comfortable with the ones they are with. If someone is comfortable with you, they will likely touch your arm or shoulder to get your attention, hug you when greeting you or putting their hand to your knee while asking if you're alright.

Physical touch, however, depends on the individual's personality so don't be bothered if someone doesn't do this even if they are comfortable with you.

I'm-Digging-This Grin or Smile

Whenever your partner is grinning or smiling madly, it means that they enjoy your conversation or are greatly interested in the topic you're talking about. If you're telling a funny story and your partner shows this kind of smile, that's a really good sign.

One Leg Tucked Underneath While on a Couch

This is a powerful comfort signal only exhibited by girls. When they feel comfortable, they usually tuck one of their legs while facing the person they're talking to. They usually do while talking and sitting on a bed or couch. Consider yourself lucky if you see this signal.

Discomfort Signals Field Guide

Identifying discomfort signals along with comfort signals will help you manage personal interactions. Whenever you notice that you can quickly fix it, making the situation more comfortable. If the person shows comfort signals again, it means that you can rest easy.

Just like comfort signals, discomfort signals usually had patterns and can be understood in context. Whenever you see this, think carefully about both comfort and discomfort signals while trying to understand the whole context of your previous conversation.

Below is the list of most common discomfort signals that are very easy to spot.

Rubbing or Touching One's Neck

The most common kind of showing discomfort, people might touch or rub their necks whenever they are not comfortable to calm themselves. If they wear a necklace, you will notice them fiddling with it.

Rubbing or Touching One's Face

Since there are also nerve endings on the face, some people might touch their faces when trying to calm themselves. Girls playing with their hair, rubbing one's eyes, rubbing one's lips or forehead are also indicators of discomfort.

Leg Rubbing

Sometimes, a person will rub their legs, wiping off their sweaty palms on their pants whenever they are uncomfortable.

Blocking or Withdrawing

Whenever someone is uncomfortable with another person, they tend to put a considerable distance between themselves and the person they're with. If this cannot be achieved, they will put obstacles between them instead. They will even do a combination of leaning away, crossing their arms in front of their chest or crossing their legs to show their discomfort. However, they might do the latter things whenever they feel cold so make sure that you look at the context carefully.

Feet Pointed Away

Being a powerful body language signal, the position of one's feet exactly tells whether the person is comfortable or not. If someone's feet are pointed away, it means that they would want to stop or evade the ongoing discussion or topic. However, if you're seated on a cramped space such as inside an airplane, this isn't applicable. Otherwise, if you notice this signal, you might as well end the conversation.

The "Interrupting" Hand

There are times whenever someone wants to say something, they raise their hand. Looking at the context, this is not a discomfort signal but rather a sign that they're stopping themselves right before they say anything. In such a case, you might as well pause and let them speak, too.

Little or No Eye Contact

No one can always maintain eye contact , aside from the fact that doing such can be uncomfortable. However, it is also not a comfortable signal if one does little or no eye contact with their partner. Doing this could either mean that the doer is guilty of committing or hiding something.

It is only natural for someone to look at you for a few seconds while you're talking, especially if you call their names. Otherwise, it could mean that they are not comfortable talking with you.

Also, pay attention if someone is looking at someone else. Most of the time, it could mean that they want to talk to that person depending on the context. However, if you happen to ask a "Who" question beforehand, it's a different story.

CHAPTER 10:

Empathy and Mentorship

Empathy is how you perceive things the way others see them. Being empathic is putting yourself in someone else's shoes so you can understand why a person reacts the way he does in a certain period and a given situation.

Empathy allows us to relate to others in a way that we can communicate to them our ideas. It also helps us understand what the person feels as they communicate with us. It is one of the major building blocks of social interaction.

But how can you acquire empathy? How can you relate to how they feel?

To some extent, humans are designed to empathize with one another as our brains are wired to relate to the emotions that another person is experiencing in a certain situation. An example is when you witness someone hit by a baseball bat. You can't help but close your eyes or shout because you empathize with the person.

However, our levels of empathy vary and only a few have high levels of natural empathy. Some people are quick to pick up others' emotions by simply looking at them while others failed to realize that someone is angry not unless they were hit. The majority, however, understand how someone feels when they choose to.

Empathy is part inherent and partly acquired. So depending on how sensitive you are, learning how to develop empathy can mean more or less work for you.

Understanding Your Emotions

Here are some questions that you can ask yourself so you can better understand your feelings:
- Do you permit yourself to feel a certain emotion?
- Do you understand the reason behind every emotion that you feel and why are you feeling it?
- Do you think it is okay to feel that emotion?
- Do you have a healthy way of displaying your feelings?

After answering the above questions, did you get some point/s that you answered negatively or are you not sure of what you are going to answer? If you answered some questions with "no", it would be best to ponder why you answered that way and how you could empathize more with yourself. Try to confide with someone that you can put your trust and ask for advice. You can also ask for help from counselors. It's worth the time and investment so that you can have a healthy and solid emotional comprehension of yourself that will lead to a happy and healthy life.

Since we humans are emotional beings, it's good if you can have a clear understanding of your own emotions since your emotions are part of your being. If you can identify and comprehend your feelings, you can better associate with others especially in times that they are undergoing what you have previously felt or experienced. So, it's a plus factor for your relationships with other people if you can relate to what they feel even if you don't want to understand your feelings. Besides, emotions are part of them as it is part of yourself, too.

Thinking Below the Surface

This is an activity that may help you understand yourself more:

Try to keep track of whatever emotion you may feel during the day. It may be anger, frustration, etc. Then, meditate on these emotions and try to ask yourself why you felt that way in a certain situation.

For example, you got angry because you got cut off the traffic. Ask yourself why you got angry. You may answer because you got cut off but what you need to do here is to dig a little deeper on your emotions. You might answer that you feel disrespected by the other driver or you might be undergoing a hard time right now that's why you got easily angered. By thinking it through, you might even realize that you don't have a real good reason to get angry after all.

You can try different ways to understand your emotions better. You may opt for a walk at the end of the day and get time for yourself to think over the emotions that you felt during the day. You may also ask a friend or a part of your family to help you understand more by conversing with them. You may also keep track of your emotions and the reason why you felt that way by writing it down. Then, compare your records daily to find if you've got a trend and understand yourself more. Whatever results you have, it will help you understand yourself little by little each day until you can understand others also.

Understanding Others

It is quite natural for us to be self-centered as we live in a world full of people who only cared about their interests most of the time and not about the feelings of others. But do you know that exercising empathy does great wonders to your social life?

Instead of being concerned only with yourself, why not also consider how others would feel in a certain situation? Of course, this is not an easy job that you could work on overnight. It takes a lot of practice learning the habit of being concerned about others' welfare. But if you could be consistent with this habit, you could develop true empathy towards others. You would be less asking these questions and automatically be sensitive to what they are feeling.

Every time that you have a conversation, ask yourself these two questions:
- What are their thoughts and feelings about the situation?
- How do they perceive the interaction?

Of course, the chance that you might get the right answer right away is not high but at least, you could get near to the real answer.

Now, your next move should be acting on your knowledge about what they are thinking or feeling. For example, you're in a grocery store and you notice that the man on the counter greeted without enthusiasm. If you realize that the person is sad, then you could cheer him up. A smile or a little compliment can sometimes lighten up the mood. By empathizing with others, you are likewise comforting yourself.

There is also another point in showing empathy. Your actions must complement what you say – this is body language and it plays an important key in how you could develop true empathy.

Non-verbal Empathy

When trying to show your empathy, make sure that your words synchronize with your non-verbal language or non-verbal empathy. Whenever you try to empathize with others through speech, your actions must work with it.

If you ask a friend cheerfully when you think he's not in the right condition, he might think that you are insincere when you ask him about his problem. Of course, your voice should sound concerned instead of being cheerful so that he would believe that you are interested to hear what he's going to say. It might be overwhelming for you to combine both speech and action so that you can be a true empathizer. But just practice. It is just simple to learn what action would accompany what you want to say. You can put it up in two signal options. Would you be in high energy or low energy?

High and Low Energy Actions

Low energy level means you are quiet, reserved or in a relaxed state. Unlike when you are in high energy actions, you tend to get loud, excited and expressive. But not all happy persons that you see are experiencing high energy or sad persons on low energy. Commonly, a person who won the lottery may be jumping up and down in happiness but some act relaxed and not that expressive. Also, you could not define people as having high or low energy all the time. A friend of yours who feels excited at the moment may feel high energy but you should not say that he is a high-energy person because of that instance.

Empathy and Energy

It's easy to say when a person is in high or low energy state but how do you connect your actions with empathy? Let's say, you went out with a friend in a restaurant. You noticed that she is quiet and reserved (low energy) but at that time you are boisterous and you feel like partying and flirting around (high energy). You might not notice but your friend may just want to have a restful night and have a quiet chat with you. Instead, you do the opposite and start partying. This becomes the conflict and makes it harder to connect with your friend.

Energy Matches Actions

What should be your action so that you could empathize with her? Be at low energy like her. If she wants to just stay at the table, try to lower your energy and converse with her quietly. If you perceive that the other person is at high energy, be at high energy. If you think the other exhibits low energy, try to lower your energy even if you feel high energy at the moment. The key here is to be at the same level of energy with the other instead of exceeding their energy actions. When your energy levels mismatch, there are more tendencies that you are not going to understand each other.

Energy matching does not only apply individually. You can also apply it to social situations. Let's say you are in a formal occasion. It is best if you are going to be relaxed and not boisterous. Unlike in parties, you should be on high energy- in partying mood. If it happens to be your first time in a social event, be wise to consider first if the event is a low or high energy occasion. After that, adapt to the occasion. You might think that if you keep on doing this practice, your energy action is at stake. But it doesn't mean that you should always blend in the crowd nor does it mean that your energy.

The Importance of Having a Good Mentor

Mentors play a significant role in learning social skills. Usually, mentors are those social butterflies that you want to be someday.

If you intend to get out of your cocoon and fly around without fear and anxiety facing people and challenges in life, you need a mentor to guide you. Mentors are those people who have been there ahead of you. They have acquired social skills because they may have been subjected to the same hardship in life.

You can expect a mentor to be strong which is why they can come out unscathed after having been through hard times.

You need people like them so you can learn from their experiences. It would be a shortcut for you. Mentors are the best ones from whom you can learn how to transform yourself into a social butterfly because they have experienced everything - even those things you haven't experienced yet.

Finding, therefore, a good mentor will make things easier for you to achieve your good of acquiring the needed social skills.

CHAPTER 11:

Ordinary People

While we are social beings, every day we deal with people and make the most out of our everyday connections is so easy. Every day we are confronted with opportunities to meet people where relationships can start from a simple conversation. All that we need to do is to connect with ordinary people that we happen to meet every day on person-to-person interaction and not on a functional one.

But how do we differentiate these two types of interactions?

Functional Interactions

When you go out and ride a bus, you are communicating with the bus driver. This is a functional interaction. When you go to a bookstore and buy a book, you interact with the bookstore owner and this is also a functional interaction.

When your interaction with these people is limited to business transactions, you are missing the chance to connect with them on a more personal level which means that you are missing other opportunities as well. It does not need to be that way.

Person-to-Person Connection

When you go beyond the functional interaction level, you are allowing the real connection to take place. Maybe a smile will do or say,

"I enjoy reading books which I bought from your store and it has become a habit!"

As you acknowledge his presence beyond being just someone who sells books, the other person may be able to extend warmth and gratitude in return and from there, a simple connection may eventually turn into a real friendship.

Every day of your life, you encounter people you meet every day and yet you never have the chance to know them personally aside from meeting them on the street, sitting side by side with them on the bus, or passing by them as they sell something on the sidewalk where you used to pass by.

To improve your social skills, spare a minute to greet the person you happen to recognize by face or give a genuine smile to the little girl selling flowers or newspapers by the sidewalk.

There are boundless opportunities to connect with people. Just make a little effort to recognize the personhood of persons you often meet on your way home from work and you will find more connections you never thought possible.

Person-to-person connections are a powerful tool to use in connecting with others. Nonetheless, it can take time before you can feel more comfortable to be with them. But like other social skills, practice makes perfect and before you know it, you are connecting to more people than you expect.

In connecting, take the following tips in mind.

Some People are not Comfortable Connecting

Not all people find connecting on a person-to-person level comfortable. When you ask something to a person next to you on a bus or grandstand while watching a ballgame and they answer you with a one-word reply, take it as that person is not someone who is sociable. Respect their desire to be alone and leave them on their own. It is important to recognize if a person wants to connect or not.

Once you have recognized that the person is not interested in connecting with you, simply back off to avoid irritating them. Be quick to spot the different comfortable and uncomfortable signals. When you detect a sign of discomfort, it's a sign that the person prefers not to talk.

Avoid Distracting People

When attempting to connect with someone, make sure that they are not in the middle of any activity so you won't be distracting them. It would be comfortable for them and easier for you to attempt.

Not All Connections Turn to Friendship

Not all the people you connect with will turn out to be a friend. You may be connecting with the store or grocery owner in the neighborhood but they may not necessarily be your friends. After buying something from them and exchange a few words, you can go home. This kind of interaction is not expected to turn into a relationship but still considered a positive interaction.

Person-to-person connections are your portal to a richer life and if you're making them a part of your everyday life, your life will be a lot different from the one you previously had.

Section 3

How to Improve Your Social Skills

CHAPTER 12:

Starting Off Slow

Have you ever experienced engaging in a conversation with someone and yet you feel you two aren't connecting? It is because you are communicating in entirely different levels of communication. This chapter will focus on how to start developing social skills and so you must know the different levels of communication.

Social Level

This level is superficial but useful, especially when approaching a stranger. It also allows you to determine if a person is an enemy or could-be friends. In this level of communication, you care to talk about just anything under the sun like the weather, news, sports, etc.

Mental Level

In the second level, you may talk about plans, ideas, facts, non-controversial beliefs, as well as tips and strategies. This is where we converse professionally. To most people, this level of communication is too important that they spend plenty of resources to ensure that they communicate best at this level.

It is on this level that battles of wits occur. People communicating on this level believe that they are better learned, smarter, wittier, and never go wrong.

There is a narrow chasm between the first and second levels. A polite conversation can easily transform into a mentally stimulating interaction and quickly get back to a polite one. These first two levels of communications are quite safe except from the context of communication wherein one party would want to impress the other.

Emotional Level

On this level, we would discuss our needs, wants, joys, fears, and aspirations. It is at this level where lips quiver, voices fail, eyes rolled or welled up, and chest up. There are many more to this list. As this level is all about transparency, trust, intimacy, and vulnerability, the gap between the first two levels and the third is quite wide.

The majority of us are terrified to face any form of rejection, hence; we are afraid to commit mistakes. Communicating at the emotional level paves the way to experience rejection, heartaches, and left emotionally scarred. This can be worse for men when they consider an open display of signs of emotional communication for them is a sign of being weak.

It's an irony that many people yearn for emotional connection and yet are avoiding it. We spend many hours talking about inert ideas and we rarely talk about our wants, dreams, joys, and needs. The emotional level of communication lays the basis upon which relationships, families, groups, peers, comrades, and societies are built.

Spiritual Level

This is not easy to talk about as our everyday mindset and language fail to readily acknowledge it. Only a few people can sink in into this level as this is the absolute highest level of resonance – no distortion from social, emotional or mental games.

Communication at a deeper level takes intention, trust, and time. It's easy to be inadequate on these three elements for various reasons, but they're something to spring on people who aren't ready to experience it.

CHAPTER 13:

One Mouth and Two Ears

While it is good to talk with someone, remember that communication is a two-way process. When you are not expressing yourself, then it's the time when you need to actively listen to what the other person is saying. How would you feel when the words you are saying fell on plugged ears and so you need to should just so they can hear you?

Why do you think we are provided with two ears and just one mouth?

According to a Greek Stoic, Epictetus:

> *"We have two ears and one mouth so we can listen twice as much as we speak."*

Why Do We Need to Listen?

Active listening is important in any communication. So when you engage yourself in any interaction, actively listening can have its benefits.

- You can learn more about the person you are in interaction with
- You can easily understand other people's ideas and emotion
- You can communicate more smoothly
- It is easy to respond with empathy and sensitivity
- You can appear to be more polite and the other person can feel that you value them and their ideas.

The Art of Active Listening

To practice the art of active listening, consider the following ways to help you improve your communication skills.

Give Your Full Attention

Try not to engage in any unnecessary movements that will take your attention away from the one speaking. Avoid looking and playing with your mobile phone or fiddle with your hands while someone is talking.

Show that you are attentively listening and are interested in what is being said. It's not enough that you are only listening. You must understand everything that's passing through your ears. It is for this reason why your ears are attached to your head so information passing through it can be processed through your brain.

You can show people that you are interested in what is being relayed to you by making eye contact with the speaker and asking questions. This will encourage them more to open up and feel comfortable expressing themselves.

Respond to Interact

It is important to give feedback while interacting. This is called "reflective listening." It is about giving feedback to reassure the other person that you are not only listening but also understanding everything that has been said. Voicing out your opinion on what was said makes sure that you understand correctly.

Listen With Your Heart

While you listen, it is not only about attention and understanding words. There is more to understand like sensing the motive behind those words. To be able to know the sentiments of the person, you have to listen to the feelings as they are being relayed. You can do this by opening your heart as you listen.

Never Interrupt

Regardless of how agitated you felt especially when you or your idea is being criticized, never interrupt while the other person is saying something. Just because you are being criticized doesn't give you the right to simply shut down your line of communication. Wait for your turn and when it comes, make your point clearly and strongly.

Don't Try to be All-Knowing

When we are familiar with the person we are in a conversation with, we are most likely to think that we know then in and out - including what they think and feel. We are usually like this to people who are close to us. However, many arguments go around in circles as people usually jump to conclusions regarding what the other person is saying without really taking the time to listen.

Find the Right Time to Listen

Because of our hectic schedule, we often listen half-heartedly to people who are dear to us which often results in miscommunication and causes the relationship to break. To avoid this, find the right time and place to listen actively. Sometimes we only need an appropriate time and space to talk and to listen to each other to enhance the relationship.

Be Respectful

If you are communicating, regardless of who is it, you must show respect. Without it, communication can soon get dissolved. Caring about what the other says and believing that they have the right to speak and be listened to go a long way in your relationship.

Avoid Selective Listening

Miscommunication often occurs because you are only choosing messages you want to hear and words you don't want to hear automatically fall on deaf ears. Avoid practicing this lest you get used to this. It's disrespect to the other person. Don't wait that it will bounce back to you before you realize how bad it is.

Think About the Message Beyond Those Words

We listen quicker than we talk; hence, we find it frustrating to wait for someone to finish a message. Listening actively requires you to include in your attention not just hearing words but also deciphering what they mean. Every word has a different meaning and so much more with phrases and sentences. Active listening allows you to understand the right meaning for the message they want to convey to you. You don't need to respond quickly. What is important is that you say the right response when it's your turn to say your piece.

Once you have learned the skill of active listening, you will find it much easier to communicate, too. Take time to practice not only with your partner but also with other people - friends, family, and co-workers. You may believe that listening is an innate ability but it is a learned skill that needs the practice to master.

CHAPTER 14:

Giving Compliments

Giving compliments is a great way to start a conversation, reduce anxiety while connecting with people, and developing bonds. This is why it is an important part of the social skills that you need to learn as well.

Steps to Giving Great Compliments

- Don't give random compliments as they will appear to be insincere.

- Give specific compliments rather than general compliments. Instead of saying, "I like your hair!" say, "I like your hair because it's full and bouncy!"
- It's easy to start a conversation when you're either giving or receiving compliments.
- Example: "What shampoo are you using that it makes your hair looks too beautiful!"
- Make sure that when giving compliments, you consider your relationship with the person as well as the setting to be appropriate. Giving out personal comments of a personal nature must only be extended to close friends in a private setting.
- Instead of the usual words, be more creative in your choice of words. For example, "Your new hairstyle is fabulous. It emphasizes your well-chiseled facial features."
- When giving out compliments, it's best to focus on the character traits rather than on the appearance. Let's say, compliment the parent on how they raised a well-mannered kid. Give constructive criticism. People can appreciate more your compliments when they know you are the type who is honest even about faults.
- Be straightforward and never shy away from giving compliments to people in authority. It's an irony but people in power tend to receive fewer compliments. You might be surprised at the pleasant response you can receive when the person welcomes the positive comment.
- On the other hand, when giving out a compliment to someone with low esteem, avoid inflated praises. Also, compliment their behavior rather than personal characteristics. Study shows that children with low self-esteem when complimented

give them worries of failures in the future. They likewise tend to avoid future challenges.

Once you can master the art of extending compliments, you will see that you can also gracefully receive compliments. Just remember one thing, whether it's giving or receiving compliments, it must always be a POSITIVE experience!

CHAPTER 15:

Acquaintances to Friends

If you're a natural extrovert, finding and befriending other people isn't a difficult thing to do. However, if you're an introvert, doing this isn't easy even if you're already a grown-up. Unless you're a toddler, your parents won't try to find new friends for you. Doing this will make you rely on your social skills alone.

Finding and Meeting People

Meeting up with other people means that you need to get out of your comfort zone. If you're an introvert, it's only natural for you to prefer speaking up with people you already know. In other words, a place brimming with strangers can be draining as well as overwhelming. The good thing is, finding and meeting people isn't as hard as you think.

Most social events don't necessarily mean exposing yourself to a place loaded with unknown people. You just need to find people or groups of people that somehow synchronize or fits your preferences and personality to be your potential friends. Identifying the groups that fit you will make finding and meeting people easier.

In addition to that, you are not bound by a law that requires you to meet and make friends during social gatherings and events. Potential connections in the future could appear almost everywhere, whether it be inside the classroom, park, playground, mall, etc. Learning to take advantage of potential connections will reward you richly afterward.

There are three known ways for you to find these people:
- Finding them through your ideal group
- Finding through Everyday Connections
- Finding through person-to-person connections

Finding Friends Through Groups

The most natural way for people to find and meet new friends is through joining social groups. This method may be helpful at times. However, social groups aren't created equal so joining a group that doesn't fit you will just make it hard for you to find and make new friends. It may sound obvious but people usually miss this bare fact.

Sometimes, people join or sign up for groups half-heartedly, eventually finding themselves stuck in rather boring groups and making their relationship or social life unfruitful. Once they make it hard to find connections, their self-confidence withers along with their desire to socialize with other people. After a few failed attempts, they eventually return to their comfort zone and give up on making new friends.

Listed below are tips for you when identifying your ideal group.

Look for Groups Based on Something you Love to Do

Whether it is gaming, music, books or movies, you must find groups that share the same passion that you have. That way, you will become more encouraged to interact with them. You can either find this kind of people online or offline. If you rather want to meet new friends offline, you can go to places that you can potentially share your passion or hobby with potential friends. If you like playing tennis, go to a tennis court. If you like reading history books, going to the history section of your school or public library in your town or city will do the trick.

Look for Groups Where Your Close Friends Are Active Members

If your close friends are involved with a particular group, you can also take the chance to find new friends there as long as it's a good one. There are times that even your close friends will get involved with bad ones due to various circumstances such as schools or personality so involving yourself with the same group won't do you any good. If it is a good one, you can just ask your close friends to introduce you to the group, which is not needed most of the time.

Look for Groups That Meet Regularly

Making new friends as well as maintaining connections requires constant contact. To make things clear, if you want to make new friends and keep them, it's only natural for you to meet and spend time with them regularly. Keep in mind that even the closest of friends slowly drift away if they didn't meet for a long time.

Look for Groups that will let you Improve and Share your Skills

It may be a good thing to get involved in a group and make new friends. However, it is way much better if the group you're in lets you improve your other skills aside from social skills. It is also a plus if you can share your skills in that group without inhibitions of any kind.

Finding Friends Through Everyday Connections

In addition to Group connections, you can also find and meet new friends through everyday connections. If you're brave enough to start a short conversation, you can start talking to the salesclerk or security guard in your local supermarket or even to that janitor who always keeps your apartment clean. You can achieve this on a person-to-person and not just functional level as long as you don't take much of their working time.

Functional interaction refers to interactions done to people in a rather systematic way. It is just like meeting or greeting people just because you need to do something that requires their aid. For example, when you're lost inside a big city, you can just ask the policeman or a local for directions. Another example is whenever you buy your favorite coffee inside the coffee shop. Doing this will require you to talk with the barista or salesclerk whenever you want to order. You may be interacting with them but that's only because you need their aid for something. This is what functional interaction is.

Finding Friends Through Person-to-Person Connections

Finding Friends through person-to-person connections can either be done directly or, for more convenience, as a level up for either Group or Everyday Connections. You can either find potential friends through the former two. Once you find and settle the right people, you can now escalate it by connecting to them personally. You can find friends by meeting them personally but, nowadays, making friends using this kind of "leveling system" is a more convenient way.

CHAPTER 16:

Body Language

In chapter 9 where we discussed body language, we learned how to understand the different body signals of other people. So when you can spot a body signal in someone that shows they are uncomfortable, then you can look for the cause of this discomfort and try removing it. When you are in a conversation with someone and their body language signal comfort, then relax and enjoy the interaction.

How about the cues you are sending the other person? Although only a few are aware of reading and analyzing body signals and cues, yet people subconsciously respond to signals of others. So if your body language emits friendliness and warmth, the person you are talking to can easily sense that feeling and can easily and warmly interact with you in the same manner you do. Conversely, if your body language shows your boredom and disinterest, the other person is likely to feel discomfort and does not desire to interact with you.

Another thing that you must be aware of when conversing with other people is when your body language and your words don't agree.

Most of the time, we are just concerned with the words we say and forget that our body communicates things we aren't saying.

When we think we keep things to ourselves and cover them up with beautiful lies, our body language is telling the truth.

So, like when you are smiling but your smile doesn't reach your eyes, it's easy to tell that you're not really happy or enjoying the conversation or that your thoughts are somewhere else.

When your words and body language are sending different messages, people are most likely to react to your body language. When you have no intention of sending a different message through your body language, then this is where the trouble begins.

When you are communicating, be aware of your body signals. Make sure that signals and cues sent are in coherence with your words. If these two aren't in sync and you need to alter one to suit your intention, then you should change your words instead of your words. However, remember that when you do this, you are either deceiving someone or yourself and deception never lasts long. Relationships that include deception will never provide you with long-term satisfaction and intimacy.

Being aware of the message sent by your body language including gesture, posture, facial expressions, and even way of walking ensures you that you are saying words that truly reflect the truth and not deception.

Awareness of the different body language signals and cues will make you aware of how to deal with people you are interacting with.

CHAPTER 17:

Tone of Voice

Your tone of voice expresses the way you think and the values you hold. It shouldn't, in any way, be considered lightly if you want to improve your social skills. Depending on the tone of your voice, it can incite various emotions such as hurt, anger, disappointment, inspiration, or interest.

The Significance of the Tone of Voice and Why You Should Develop It

Your tone gives you the opportunity to present your best self. If you want to attract friends and broaden your social circle, you should learn how to use the tone of your voice according to your current social setting. For instance, you're with your colleagues or potential business partners. Your tone should be professional, authoritative, and persuasive at the same time. If you're in a barbecue party, it should be light-hearted and melodic which insinuates that you're enjoying their company. At the same time, having the same consistent tone over time will help you build your brand. Make sure that it's likable and natural. Again, make your voice reflect your inner values.

It Distinguishes You

Communicating quietly, angrily, or passionately can generate an impact on how people interpret you. If voice and tone weren't considered, all of us might sound monotonous and unenergetic. Your uniqueness wouldn't even be recognized by others, and vice versa. The tone of voice can convey your sense of humor, warmth, competence, or any attribute that you want to project and makes you memorable to the people you meet.

It Helps You Gain and Build Trust

People can identify your personality based on the tone of your voice. They start to configure an image of a person based on the present. By doing this, people are given the opportunity to get to know you; thus, bringing with it a sense of familiarity and trust. Developing a consistent tone of voice helps you project authenticity and to some extent, sincerity.

You Can Utilize It to Influence and Persuade

Your voice is a great tool to influence and persuade people—whether it may be in a romance, friendship, or business partnership. Its potency is also heightened when you also choose the right words at the right time. Observe how actors or public speakers deliver their lines or messages. Their tone varies as they try to put power behind the words they say. Aside from their facial expressions, this is how they move the hearts of their audience. This isn't to say that you need to put on a show or something. What you need is to get the idea of how you can make an impact on people using the tone of your voice.

It Helps You Create Good First Impressions

We all know how first encounters can be crucial. People don't merely assess your appearance or behavior, but also with other non-verbal cues including the tone of your voice. A soft voice conveys that the person talking is timid, shy, and lacks self-confidence. On the flip side, a person with a loud, booming voice lets you know that they are aggressive or have a strong personality. If you want to make a new acquaintance, speak slowly but not to the point of monotony. The other person should still see that you're interested in making their acquaintance.

How Can You Improve Your Tone of Voice?

Communication can be a challenge. Yes, using words and body language may be adequate at times. However, if you truly want to put power in every message and even enhance your communication style, we suggest that you improve the tone of your voice. On the other hand, using the wrong tone can create problems. You might be familiar with the lines: *"Don't you use that tone with me!"* or *"The problem doesn't lie with your words but how you deliver them."*

When you pay little attention to the tone of your voice, you are also neglecting the potential of your presence. You are restraining the potential of your communication, something which we don't want to, especially when we're aiming to improve our social skills. To help you with, we listed five types of voice tones and some key points on how to apply them to enhance your communication style.

First Type: Command and Questioning Tonality

You may not be conscious of the impact of your voice tone or whether you're using the right tone for your message. A voice tone can be mismatched to what you're saying. You could be saying one thing but others hear a very different thing. You may be using a commanding tone while you're merely asking a question or vice versa.

A command tonality should project authority (and at times, intimidation); whereas, a questioning tonality conveys uncertainty (and of course, lacks authority) in your communication.

Vocal Tips:
- When using command tonality, use a deeper pitch and lower frequency. Your voice should sound strong that conveys authority and drop the intonation at the end of your sentence.
- When using questioning tonality, use a higher frequency, pitch, and intonation. It should also be softer, brighter, and involves more breath.

Both tonalities should be controlled and definitely shouldn't be your consistent voice tone since they can restrict your presence and may negatively affect how others perceive you. You must know when to utilize these tones depending on the conversations or interactions you are in.

Second Type: Friendly Tone

A friendly tone is what we often use particularly when we're with friends or people we want to be friends with. We don't want our "friendly tone" to be intimidating, sarcastic, or offending. However, because we have different personalities, we may have used a very different kind of friendly tone in the process. We can only learn from each other by imitating the tones we like and see if it fits us.

Vocal Tips and Practice:
- A friendly tone is usually pitched higher, not deeper. It's not aggressive or loud but more relaxed and breathier. Your vocal cords shouldn't be pressured or tightly closed, but free of tension to allow the breath to flow more easily.
- To discover your own unique friendly vocal tone, start by asking yourself what a friendly tone sounds like.

- You can play with your voice by doing some acting. Record your voice (or video record everything) so you can review it afterward. Remember, your tone should be higher than usual but not loud or high-pitched.

Third Type: Tone for Compliments

To sound thankful and sincere, you should use a breathier and brighter vocal tone, though you shouldn't overdo it. Typically, we trust and feel safe when we detect sincerity in the tone.

Fourth Type: Tone for Urgency

When you want to be heard because of a pressing issue, you must use a stronger deeper tone with less breath. This way, your audience will understand that you mean what you say. This tone quality demands attention and you will surely get it.

Fifth Type: Tonality for Business (Particularly for Women)

The ability to make more money is generally linked with individuals with deeper voices. This is because of the perception that deeper tone quality conveys authority and assertiveness which are characteristics essential in business. With this, women who typically have high-pitched voices are at a disadvantage. Their voice quality sounds less certain in a business environment.

A command tonality is one of the leadership skills and women who have higher-pitched voices usually struggle to create this quality. Vocal exercises can help women strengthen and improve their voice. Margaret Thatcher, former British Prime Minister, was a good example of how her effectiveness as a leader had improved after taking vocal lessons.

CHAPTER 18:

Keeping With the Conversation

Whenever someone has an enjoyable conversation, the chances are that those conversations naturally move from one topic to another and one speaker to the next one. Since it's somewhat instinct, there's no need for you to think about what to say or talk about next. Instead of worrying about the entire conversation flow, you can just enjoy the time spent on it.

Conversation flow happens during a comfortable, effortless and smooth conversation. It is the way conversations are supposed to go. Most of the time, if you're comfortable with the person you're with, conversation flow happens naturally. However, if this doesn't happen, the principle of invitation and inspiration comes in. These two are the key and most important ingredients of conversation flow.

Invitation and Inspiration

An invitation is something you say that lets your partner know and get the signal that it is their turn to speak. An inspiration, on the other hand, is something you say that makes your partner speak even without giving them the signal. These two keep the conversation flowing.

With practice, you will realize that both invitation and inspiration are useful whenever you are in a conversation, which makes it more enjoyable.

To illustrate, let's say you are walking home with someone who happens to be living near you but you were not that close. But because you see each other almost every day on your way to work and back home, it would be impolite not to acknowledge her. To do this, your opening would be something like,

"Hi, our schedule happens to be the same."

"I notice, too. So, how's your work?"

"Fine!"

Notice that when you respond to the question with "fine", you are cutting the conversation and so the conversation stopped. But if you followed it with a leading question, the other person will be encouraged to continue with the conversation.

"It's fine, how about you?"

With this response, the other person will take it as an invitation to go on with the conversation. Either way, using a leading question lets your partner know that he is invited to continue with the interaction and it also signals him that it turns to keep the conversation flowing.

Invitation and Inspiration

Invitations are useful since it protects your conversations from stopping abruptly. It can also be used as a tool for building intimacy and rapport with the one you're talking with. However, even though invitations are quite handy, it is not enough to build an entire conversation using those. Doing it will make the conversation looks like an interview with awkwardness on the side.

Keep in mind that conversation flow comes from one speaker to the next, sometimes with invitations in between.

Inspiration in Good Conversation

Good or great conversations both need invitation and inspiration. If a conversation composed of invitations sounds like a job interview, conversations composed of inspirations are somewhat close to impossible. Just think of yourself trying to inspire your partner but they didn't respond. Sound awkward, right?!

The best solution in conversation flow is to move smoothly between invitation and inspiration, depending on the conversation needs. While invitations add structure and guidance to conversations, inspirations add flexibility and intimacy. In other words, you can start the conversation by giving off invitations before inserting inspirations as the conversation flows smoothly. If in case that the person isn't responding to the inspiration or the conversation becomes somewhat uncomfortable or awkward, kindly revert to using more invitations until the conversation flows again.

When the conversation starts, you should use invitations more frequently, especially if you don't know the person well or if your partner doesn't know what to say next. On the other hand, use inspirations more frequently if you already know the person very well and if they happen to share or ask something personal to you. Keep in mind that conversation flow is affected by the persons' intimacy level. Needless to say, the more you know the person, the deeper you can dig or involve yourself in their personal lives without making them uncomfortable.

The Core of the Good Conversation

People feel comfortable in sharing stories without an invitation when conversation flows smoothly and naturally. They feel encouraged and will chime in whenever they want to share something.

To create a good conversation flow, you should remember these two things: Inspire your partner to share and make them comfortable in sharing as much as possible.

To make your partner comfortable, be friendly and pay attention to their body language signals. To know them better, give good invitations to encourage them to share more.

You can make a conversation by using nothing but invitations. However, unless you're doing some kind of activity like inventing or painting something, it will be rather awkward and look like a job interview. In addition to that, something done out of inspiration is more creative and emotive than something done out of trading invitations or suggestions. And last but not least, both people will have more fun and will be closer to each other.

Inspiration also does wonders when used in a conversation. Through inspiration, you and your partner will be encouraged to share your stories as the conversation flows smoothly and naturally, eventually making you closer to each other. In other words, you are being inspired by people you talk to if whatever they share also makes you want to share something with them as well.

Just by definition, inspiration doesn't make you or anyone feel compelled to share; rather, it gives them the desire or wants to share. When you inspire someone, you encourage and welcome them to share without giving them a sense of obligation to do it. It also gives them more freedom when sharing or responding to the topic. Compared to the invitation, inspiration allows room for more elaborate explanations rather than short and quick answers.

Weaving inspiration to conversations frees yourself from the responsibility of what to say during your next turn. By creating a conversation flow together, inspiration encourages both you and your partner to know each other more deeply. There is no need for both of you to memorize a prepared script. Rather than that, you just need to be genuine whenever you share something and share it in a way that will encourage your partner to share as well.

Harmonizing Invitation and Inspiration

It is a well-known fact that invitation and inspiration are both needed to make a great conversation. If a conversation made out of invitations makes it look like a job interview, a conversation made out of inspiration is almost impossible to do. In addition to that, both of you will look awkward, especially if your partner didn't respond to any of it.

Depending on the needs of the conversation, one must learn how to move between invitation and inspiration smoothly. If the invitation adds the structure, inspiration, on the other hand, adds intimacy and flexibility during a conversation. The general rule is to start a conversation by giving away invitations and use more inspirations as the conversation flows and progresses smoothly. If you notice a rather awkward pause done by your partner, return to using invitations until the conversation is flowing smoothly once again.

To say it simply, use more inspiration when it seems like it is the appropriate thing to do but don't be afraid to give invitations whenever necessary. Use invitations at the start of the conversation and when your partner doesn't know what to share next, especially if you happen to know each other firsthand. Use inspiration if you know your partner much better and if they happen to share or ask you about something personal. Keep in mind, though, that both cannot be accomplished in just one conversation.

CHAPTER 19:

100 Questions

Remember here that our goal is to keep things going in a conversation so you will never run out of things to say on your first encounter.

Conversations flow when they naturally move from one topic to another while encouraging a smooth exchange of words from two or more speakers. This is the primary goal when it comes to improving one's social skills.

Invitation: The Art of Good Questioning

To encourage conversation flow, one of the primary tools used is none other than invitation. An invitation is something you say that encourages the one you're speaking with to interact by speaking what's inside their minds. This also gives your partner a suggestion on what to talk about next. Questions such as "What did you do?" or "What do you for a living?" are examples of an invitation.

Invitations are some kind of a safety net whenever someone encounters rough spots during a conversation. If you're clueless on what to do talk next, you can invite to keep the conversation flowing. It's ideal to throw out an invitation that is related to the previous discussion, though it's not essential. Keep in mind that, even though most invitations come in the form of questions, not all questions can be considered good invitations.

Good Questions

When encouraging conversation flow, you should just ask good questions which, in this case, are open-ended ones. Open-end questions are invitations that allow your partner to talk for a while instead of being limited to a rather short answer or simply Yes or No. If you want your conversation to flow, short and one-word responses are not ideal.

If you ask questions in an open-ended way, it will encourage your partner to share his thoughts or experiences. For example, if you ask your partner, "What did you do last weekend?" it's only natural for them to give out a lengthy reply that will keep the conversation flow.

This also allows you to show your interest in the person in a way that is not too invasive of their personal life. By asking such insightful questions, it tells your partner that you want to know them much better. Because if it isn't like that, there is no way that you will ask such a question in the first place. Not only will it tell your partner that you're interested in them; it will also show that you are concerned about their well-being.

Asking Good Questions

Asking good and insightful questions can also be considered an art. Asking a very superficial question such as "What do you think of today's weather?" will not help you find out something about that person as well as it will not tell them clearly that you're interested or concerned. However, it will let you get closer to them while opening the opportunity for conversation flow. On the other hand, asking an intimate question such as "Do you have a dark secret?" firsthand will not just make the person uncomfortable; they will probably take it as your offense against them.

The trick to making the conversation flow is to start asking superficial questions, and then slowly ask more intimate questions depending on the flow of the situation. If in case the other person shows some kind of discomfort, ask less intimate questions to lighten up the mood. However, if they are still comfortable, you can continue digging deeper by asking more questions.

There are two things that you need to keep in mind.

First, the progression from asking superficial questions to intimate ones does take time, meaning that you can't accomplish it in just one conversation. Intimate questions can only be answered by those who have a close relationship with you. So whenever you meet someone firsthand, it's only natural for you to ask something about the weather before digging deeper into their lives by asking their names and workplace. As time goes by and after lots of conversations from that particular person, you can then start asking more intimate questions as you know each other more than before. This only happens after you have shared many comfortable conversations.

Second, if you ask intimate questions to that person, you should be prepared to answer intimate questions yourself. You can consider this as a "give and take" matter. If you want the other person to open up to you, you should learn to open up to them. Otherwise, it will make them uncomfortable.

CHAPTER 20:

The Group Game Begins

We have laid out the foundation for good conversation in the previous chapter and since we know that most interactions take place in a group, so in this chapter we concentrate on the principles behind group conversations.

As much as it is important to discern if you are acceptable to a person you are approaching, the more that you must be able to discern if you are acceptable to a group. It is by reading the group's body language that you discern if the group is open or closed to new members. To be able to do this, you must know the different key signals that will show you if the group is open or not.

Joining Group Conversation

When you can identify a group that eagerly welcomes others to join them, you have to walk in and participate in the conversation. To make this easier, we have to teach you here on how to participate in group conversations as you join in.

To join in, you have to make sure that you won't hamper the smooth flow of the ongoing conversation. To do this, you have to know how to speak up in a conversation.

Open and Closed Groups

To participate in a group is easier said than done. You may have walked in a social event and find everyone bunched up in small groups and you find yourself in a loss especially when you are a newcomer. No one would be there to usher you or invite you to join in and there's no other solitary newcomer you can cling to. Standing alone and undecided is a real bummer and you feel walking out of there could be the best thing. So what would you do?

When you are in this kind of situation, the first thing to do is not to panic. Take a moment to observe before rushing in to join a group. First, categorized groups into either open or closed groups.

An **open group** is approachable for a newcomer like you while a closed group is an exact opposite. By merely looking at their member's body language, you can easily tell what type of group it is.

For a **closed group**, members tend to move closer, with almost no gaps in between group members as they turn directly towards each other. They aren't necessarily unfriendly and the situation may change later and they can become open. It's just that they are currently contented with the number of people joining in the conversation and have no interest in allowing more people to join in. The topic they may be discussing for the moment could be sensitive enough or it could be that they are busy discussing that they don't have time to entertain newcomers. Rarely would a group intentionally close themselves but and you can easily detect a close group with the desire to be left alone through its members' body language. In this case, it's best to respect the signals their sending and choose instead groups that are more open and approachable.

Open Groups

These are groups that are more open to newcomers and people can just come and go. Have this group as your target. Like the closed groups, you can easily spot an open group through the body language of its members. However, an open body language may differ depending on the number of people in a group.

Being open or closed is not limited to groups as individuals can likewise be open or closed. You can easily spot **an open person** as he will be facing the crowd and busy like the others – with face, feet, and torso pointing towards the crowd or the center of the room. You may also notice that they are quite alert and excited while ready for someone to approach them.

Conversely, a close person tends to look down, away from the group, either facing the door or doing something to look busy such as texting or reading a book. However, don't be fooled by this since there are also individuals who love to be approached. It's just that they don't have the confidence to appear open to approaches. So, as long as you are cautious in your approach, it's fine to come to a closed individual. Be observant of their body language as well and be ready to back off if you sense that they don't want their privacy intruded.

For **two to three people in a group**, notice how they face one another. When they are facing each other directly, they are more like to be a closed group, but if members are positioned in a way that they are angled, this group may be easier to approach.

To now where a person is facing, simply look at their face, feet, and torso and determine where they are pointed at. It's usual to see two persons with faces facing each other with feet and torsos facing where most people are. The more member in that group with face, feet, and torso pointing away from other group members, the stronger indication that the group is open and will be willing to take you in.

For **large groups** or those exceeding three groups, pay more attention to the shape of the group. Open groups tend to have large gaps between members that you can easily walk through. You can walk in through a gap that forms like a horseshoe and join the conversation.

You may also spot large groups in public spaces – or activity at a social event where everyone is welcomed like a bonfire when you are camping.

Joining a Group

Finding the right group to join is easy when you know how to read a person or a group's body language. However, make sure to be attentive to the group's body language even after you have joined in. If they close off or turn away from you, then they're not really that open and you should get away from there to find a group that is more willing to accept you. If the groups remain open after you have joined in, you can relax and join in the conversation. It may not be easy to jump in into their conversation, but with little practice, you may soon easily jump in!

CHAPTER 21:

How to Successfully End a Conversation

There are conversations that you want to end because it must have taken much of your time, you are not interested in the topic, or you simply want to get away from the person you are talking to. Because you don't want to appear rude or impolite, you need to find ways to get out of there without hurting the person's ego. Here are tips on how to do it.

Tell the Other Person Directly

Sometimes, it's good just to say that you need to go without the need to explain or be guilty of it. People will understand if you have to go especially when the conversation is not scheduled and you just happened to see each other accidentally. A simple, "I have to go." will do or "I'll talk to you some other time."

Give Reasons

If you're the type who would feel uneasy leaving someone behind when you know they want to talk with you, then it's best to tell them the reason why you need to go.

"It's nice talking to you, but someone is expecting me. I'll call you when I'm free."

"Sorry, but I can't stay. I am attending an important event."

"I love to stay longer but I have to pick up my daughter in her school. Maybe we can set this some other time."

Use Non-verbal Language

So as not to appear impolite, you can start adjusting your body language and gestures to signal the other person that it's time for you to go.

- Stand up if you have been sitting down while engaging in the conversation
- Give quicker and shorter responses
- Look at your watch or check your cellphone

If you are in your work station when the other person engaged you in a conversation, show them signs that you need to get back to your work by looking at your computer or start doing something to let you know that you need to resume work.

Section 4

Improving Your Skills Depending on the Situation

CHAPTER 22:

Dating

Romance always starts with dating and dating can be wonderful. However, it can also be destructive if you start with the wrong foot.

There are many unhealthy relationships out there that prove to be disastrous because people have different personalities and behaviors. If you are not careful of whom to date with, you may end up dating the wrong person and that's where relationship issues may arise.

Before you get into this mess, let's start knowing more about dating for even a little knowledge goes a long way in avoiding these issues.

Defining Healthy Relationships

It's easy to go out dating someone you don't know in the first place. If you are interested in a person, the best way to know them more is to date them. However, dating and relationships are not all fun and sparks. They can always shift from good to worse and it could be late before you know it.

So let's take time to learn about the foundation of a healthy relationship.

A healthy relationship is something that is not abusive or manipulative. It is based on love and respect. It is giving and receiving - not less, not more!

To have a happy and fulfilling romance, consider these principles.

Sense of Acceptance and Freedom

You can tell that a relationship is healthy when you feel fully accepted and still maintain that sense of freedom. You remain as someone you originally are and not someone changed and molded to be someone who you aren't.

If you are loved by your partner, then they must be willing to accept you for what you are and not dictate what you should do just to please them. Dating and relationship is an equal partnership, so no one must be above the other especially when you are still on the dating stage.

When you feel free and accepted, there's no reason for you to hide anything from your partner. This does not mean, however, that your partner needs to approve everything that you do. They may speak up to let you know if there's something they don't approve of, but the choice is still up to you and so with them.

Opinions must be shared equally between the two of you and you must not feel that you need their permission in making decisions for yourself. Nonetheless, even when there's some disagreement, respect must remain a balancing element.

Every time a relationship issue arises, make sure that you gently talk about resolving it quickly.

Live Outside the Relationship

While dating or in a relationship, you still have individual lives outside the relationship. In a healthy relationship, both can still maintain close friendships with their circle of friends and each can support these significant parts of their lives that are outside their dating relationship.

When people start dating, there is this tendency to focus on the relationship and cut off ties with friends as the new relationship begins to take up all of their time. This kind of relationship is unhealthy.

You should maintain other social activities as well as your hobbies, social interaction with friends, improving yourself, and the likes. Healthy relationships are not limited to a world where there are only two of you. Both of you should encourage each other to go on with your life outside the relationship as there are other important things and people aside from your partner.

Shared Act of Selflessness

Being in a relationship directs you to only one goal - to give although a relationship like communication is a two-way process - give and receive.

Because LOVE in its essence is GIVING, that is why your goal is to focus on giving what you can give and not on receiving what you can get. However, a relationship needs BALANCE to be healthy. So when one party is receiving more than what he or she can give, the balance is broken and the relationship becomes unhealthy.

Taking advantage of what you can get from your partner is not love. Same thing when you please your partner to the extent that you are losing your freedom and happiness. Things like these are elements of an unhealthy relationship that must end sooner.

So before this can happen to you, be on alert for signs that could lead you to an unhealthy relationship while still on your dating stage.

Starting a Romantic Relationship

Learning the difference between a healthy and unhealthy relationship gives you the edge over others who plunge into a relationship not knowing about this. Let's start our journey to finding a romantic partner.

Meeting Potential Romantic Partners

You should meet your romantic partner just like the way you meet a new friend. Looking for a partner intentionally is more likely to end you up with an unsuitable one. When you have this intention, you are more apt to focus on creating a good impression instead of getting to know the person better. It's best to take your time knowing the other person before thinking of them as a possible romantic partner.

Real Attraction

It's natural to be attracted to someone with good looks and a pleasant character but remember that people are hiding something inside. You'd better find out what's in hiding. Attraction can either be real or physical just like fear.

If you want to be sure that what you're feeling is real attraction and not just a physical one that may easily vanish in less time, then take time known the real person behind the person. You should like the person for who they are not for what they have. Remember that it takes time to build true attraction.

Taking the time to get to know the other person will result in a solid romance, which is the foundation of LOVE - the real attraction. Love, at first sight, maybe fun and exciting, but only a few last long enough to be recognized as real. It can easily diminish as soon as the romantic sparks fade away.

CHAPTER 23:

Boundaries

To maintain self-worth, learning to set healthy personal boundaries is crucial. It can be our way of communicating with other people that we value self-worth, have self-respect, and don't allow others to defile us.

When we talk of personal boundaries, it covers the physical, mental, and emotional limits we establish to protect ourselves from being manipulated, exploited, and even abused by others. These boundaries allow us to express ourselves as someone unique and valuable in the same way that we acknowledge the same in others. Without the existence of personal boundaries, it is not possible to achieve and enjoy healthy relationships.

To achieve a healthy relationship, you must recognize that each of us is unique and has distinct needs, emotions, and preferences. To set personal boundaries means to preserve your integrity while taking control of your life and be responsible for who you are as an individual.

How to Establish Healthy Personal Boundaries

Whether you are in a relationship or not, it is important to establish a healthy personal boundary and here are ways to do it effectively.

Know Your Rights

Aside from your rights to establish personal boundaries, you must likewise take responsibility for how you allow other people to treat you. Your boundaries serve as filters separating what is acceptable or not in your life. If you don't have a clear-cut definition of these boundaries, you tend to get your sense of worth from others. To avoid these, set clear and decisive limits and make them known to others so they will learn to respect them. Make sure that you are willing to enforce them no matter at what cost. It's been proven that people with weak boundaries are more likely to violate other people's boundaries.

Identify Unacceptable Actions and Behaviors

Don't fail to let others know when they have crossed your boundaries. Also, do not be ashamed or afraid to tell others when you need physical or emotional space. Do not allow others to put pressure on you and be ready to take action once somebody violates your boundaries.

Trust Yourself

Before you put your trust in others, you have to put your full trust in yourself. No other knows you more than you do – your needs, wants, desires, values, principles, and perspectives. Don't allow anyone to trample on your beliefs or make decisions for you. Healthy boundaries make it possible for you to maintain self-trust and self-worth while respecting individuality. An unhealthy imbalance can occur once you encourage neediness, dependence on someone, or when you choose to play the victim.

Spot Signs of Unhealthy Boundaries

- When you lose the balance between giving and receiving

- When you want to please others to the extent that you are suffering
- When you know you are being exploited by others and you do nothing because you need attention
- When you are being manipulated or vice versa
- When touching a person without asking
- You feel bad saying "No" so you say "Yes" all the time even when you don't like to do it.
- Not speaking up when you are abused or treated poorly
- You are expecting others to automatically provide your needs

When you possess healthy personal boundaries, you are more likely to:

- More confident and have an improved and healthy self-concept.
- You are better and more comfortable in communicating with other people.
- You have more satisfying and fulfilling relationships
- You have more control with your life resulting in stability
- You are more in touch with nature and reality

CHAPTER 24:

Asperger's and Autism

The most important rule for learning social skills with Asperger's Syndrome is by understanding the reasons during social situations, not through rote memorization.

Rote Memorization Issues

Rote memorization is said to be the most natural way that social skills can be learned by people with Asperger's Syndrome. Through this method, people learn a specific response that can be done when a specific situation happens. For example, whenever someone tells us their name, it is only normal for us to tell them our name, too. In such a case, rote memorization is effective.

However, once the situation changes – albeit slightly, those memorized responses won't be helping at all. For example, if a friend introduces his friend to us by telling his name, is it our obligation to tell his friend our name, or is it our friend's obligation? If something like that happens, we will be at a loss for words.

It can be said that rote memorization is better than having nothing but, as always, there's also a much better way.

Learning by Understanding the Reasons Behind a Situation

Learning to understand the reasons behind a situation is much better than just memorizing specific responses whenever something happens. You must teach and train yourself to think through what to do during a certain instance and learn how to meet the expectations of other people while making the interaction more positive.

Learning this method lets you use that knowledge to derive the correct response to a certain situation, even if you don't have rote responses memorized beforehand. All you have to do is to understand what people expect from certain situations and respond in a way that matches that.

When people expect positive results from an introduction, it should include the data of everyone's names as well as relevant information concerning the people being introduced. It should also allow people to get a chance to speak, making them feel included as well as getting "a feel or vibe" for each other before the conversation begins earnestly.

We can use this knowledge to serve as a guide for our actions to know the expected results. For example, we shouldn't start telling a long story until everyone gets introduced, allowing them to speak freely first. Once we know that the introductions start a socially acceptable conversation, we can respond appropriately as someone introduces themselves to us.

The good thing about this method is that it is not just applicable to introductions; it applies to all possible situations. Once we learn the desired results that people expect from us during a social situation, we can easily choose the desirable moves. All we need to do is to think about the reasons behind the situation and deducting the things that we should be doing in that situation. This particularly frees us from the massive list of rote responses, giving us greater ability to handle almost every situation that we find ourselves in. It is simple but effective and powerful.

Practical Applications

We can apply this rule to our own lives as well. First, we should realize that no one can create a comprehensive list of desirable results at every social interaction, especially the first ones. However, we will be able to think of at least a few and we can ask our family and friends for more tips. By observing other people in various social situations, you will also be able to naturally discover more desired results. As time goes by, your understanding of social situations will grow more.

If you still encounter difficulties in understanding the whole idea, you can simply think of it as one does inside a classroom. Normally, the primary goal of having a class is for everyone to learn. A good teacher can display a list of classroom rules or he can directly teach students about those rules. Either way, the result will be the same.

You can simply think of the list of rules as Rote Memorization. Needless to say, aside from it being troublesome to memorize, there will be some situations that are possibly not listed there. It is just impossible to think of every violation that a pupil or student could ever commit and its corresponding disciplinary action. Instead of doing this, the teacher could just teach the students whether their actions will benefit or hurt others by giving a certain situation, hence letting them base their list of admirable or desirable responses and actions from those.

Keep in mind, though, that this skill only grows with practice. Even if you learn all of these, it will still not make you become a social superstar or celebrity. It takes lots of practice, time and effort to learn social skills this way.

You may somewhat say that rote memorization is better but it is not true. If reading and understanding behind social situations are a hard one, rote memorization is harder, aside from the fact that it has a very low success rate.

Learning to understand social situations also makes you learn and train to react accordingly; letting you dramatically multiply the benefits you receive from acquiring social skills. Eventually, you will find yourself becoming more able to thrive in social situations and build intimate and deep relationships with other people. This method won't make you a star in a single night but you'll be astonished by its good results over time.

CHAPTER 25:

Dealing With Children

It is common for children to have difficulties in socializing with others. For parents, this is something challenging, especially when trying to find resources that will help their struggling children. This is potentially frustrating, especially if the things that work with you don't work with their situation.

When helping children and their families improve their social skills, an evidence-based process can be done. This process can be broken down into four steps: Identification of potentially problematic social deficits, Resource Evaluation, Setting and Tracking Goals and Commencing the Work.

First Step: Problem Identification

Identifying the problem usually starts with the particular struggles that your child face such as school attendance, starting small friendships or making small or short conversations with their classmates. By identifying the problems, you will notice the social skills that need improvements.

However, the child needs to agree to cooperate with the issue at hand. Unless they cooperate, there's no way for you to identify and fix it. In other words, forcing them to cooperate will just make them think that you're invasive in their personal life.

Usually, therapists take this approach in the form of child therapy. It works by ruling out anything that will potentially affect social functions such as depression or lack of sleep before collaborating on specific social skills that need improvements. After identifying the issue, the therapists evaluate the child's strengths and weaknesses and set various short-term goals for them to accomplish.

Second Step: Resource Evaluation

Resource evaluation in regard to children's strengths and weaknesses involves determining the child's behavior with and without their families on their side or their inherent skills and talents. By spending some time with them, you can observe your child's behavior whenever you are around. On the other hand, you can just ask others about their behavior whenever you're not with them.

Aside from doing the things mentioned above, therapists also assess the personal strengths and weaknesses of parents for them to understand how the children develop their social skills at home. Once those two are determined, they can set various goals to improve the children's strengths while making them cope up with their weaknesses as they grow.

Third Step: Setting and Tracking Goals

Without setting and tracking various goals, there is no way for you to determine whether your child's social skills are progressing or regressing as time goes by. In addition to that, improving this skill requires both time and effort for both parents and children.

Sometimes, if the lack of motivation is the obstacle for a child not socializing with others, giving them encouragement as well as good motivation is your responsibility as a parent.

It is recommended for parents to collaborate with experts in child therapy when setting daily, weekly, monthly and yearly goals. Tracking these goals helps the child from getting overwhelmed or discouraged by various expectations. It is also good to adapt a reward system, meaning that the child should receive a good reward for accomplishing something that will improve their social skills. It should be in the form of something that the child desires for them to become motivated.

Both the parents and the therapist may set up regular meetings while developing strategies and monitoring the changes in children's behavior. Over time, the task or achievements may become difficult and the rewards should become greater.

Fourth Step: Let the Work Commence

After doing the three things mentioned above, it is only natural for you and your child to start working the goals out. For the work to become effective as well as productive, role-playing, support and opportunities are recommended.

Through role-playing, the child gets to experience and learn things inside a safe and monitored environment while letting you observe the process at the same time without worries. Incentives, as well as positive reinforcement for unmotivated or uninterested children, will encourage and motivate them to engage and participate in such activities, letting them improve their social skills over time. Verbal forms of encouragement are helpful but rewarding the child with something tangible is a much better method.

Working on social skills is very important for a child's overall improvement. If the goal or target is for him to make new friends, it is only natural for you to let them play outside with other children. It's just like the fact that you should go see a basketball court and game first for you to understand how it is being played.

Supporting your child is very important at this stage. Since improving social skills is somewhat difficult and problematic, there is no way for your child to accomplish it in just one try, even if he is a genius. This is also the time where the number of failures is more than successes so you need to keep your child motivated at all times. Patience is the key if you want your child to become successful in this matter.

CHAPTER 26:

Dealing With Conflicts

Conflict is a normal part of our lives. It is present even in a healthy relationship. After all, you don't expect any two people to agree with each other's ideas all the time. The key is not to avoid conflict but on how to resolve them healthily.

Conflicts that are mismanaged can cause great harm to any relationship - be it personal, in business or career. However, when handled properly, it can provide an opportunity to strengthen the bond between two people in any kind of relationship. Whatever the cause of disputes or disagreements, learning how to settle conflicts effectively through better social skills can keep your personal and professional relationship strong, growing, and healthy.

Now, let's think about the opposing need of a parent and child. A child has this need to explore and is more likely to go out and venture just to meet this need which may put the child in great danger. The parent, on the other hand, has this need to protect the child which can, of course, limit the child's desire to explore. It is at this time when a conflict arises between the parent and child.

The need for both parties is significant in the long-term success of a relationship as each deserves consideration and respect.

In personal relationships, the lack of understanding about these opposing needs may result in an argument and separation. Nonetheless, recognizing conflicting needs and facing and examining issues with understanding and compassion can lead to creatively solving the issue and creating stronger bonds.

Different Ways People Respond to Conflict

People vary in their ways of responding to conflicts. Some fear conflict and tried to avoid it at all costs. If a person's perception of conflict comes from painful and traumatic memories and experiences of their childhood or previous unhealthy relationships, then expect all conflicts and disagreement to end badly. They are sure to view conflict as something humiliating, demoralizing, or frightening. Once your early experiences had left you feeling out of control and powerless, conflict can be traumatic for you.

If you are afraid to face conflict, then it can become a self-fulfilling prophecy for you. It will be tough for you to enter a conflict situation feeling threatened or to deal with it logically. You are more to shut down instead or blow up in anger.

Emotions, Stress, and Conflict Resolution

Conflict can trigger a strong emotion resulting in disappointment, hurt feelings, and discomfort. It can also lead to resentments, break-ups, and irreparable rifts when handled poorly. Nonetheless, when effectively managed, it can help you understand more the other person while building trust and stronger ties.

Once you are out of touch with your emotions or so stressed up that you neglect to pay attention to several emotions, you will not be aware of your own needs and thus make it impossible for you to communicate effectively with other people and determine things that are troubling you.

Take for instance a couple who often argues about little things like the way he left his socks on the floor and the way she pressed the toothpaste tube instead of arguing about things that bother them.

The success of resolving any conflict depends on your ability to do the following:

- Stay alert and calm and manage your stress quickly. This will enable you to read and interpret communications accurately – both verbal and non-verbal.
- Control both your emotions and behavior. When you are in control of your emotions, you can effectively relay your needs without resorting to intimidation, threats, or punishment.
- Take heed of feelings being relayed as well as of words being expressed by others.
- Maintain respect and avoid disrespectful words and acts. This can always resolve an issue more quickly than when egos are damaged due to disrespect.

There are two significant skills you need to learn to successfully beat a conflict.

- **Quick stress relief** or the ability to quickly relieve stress instantly
- **Emotional awareness** or the ability to remain calm and be comfortable with your emotions amidst the perceived attack

Quick Stress Relief

The ability to manage and instantly relieve stress is the key to staying focused, balanced, and remain in control regardless of any challenges you are facing. If you fail to keep yourself in control and focused, there is this great tendency that you will be overwhelmed in a conflict situation and not be able to respond healthily.

There are three common ways people respond to an overwhelming situation due to stress and Connie Lillas, a psychologist described them best through the following driving analogies.

Foot on the Gas

An angry response agitated by stress making you overly emotional that you're unable to sit.

Foot on the Brake

You have this tendency to withdraw, shut down, and exhibit less emotion and energy.

Foot on Both Gas and Brake

This is a somehow tensed and frozen stress response. Once under pressure, you tend to freeze and can't do anything else. Your body seems paralyzed although, underneath it, you're highly strung.

When you are under stress, it is not easy for you to resolve conflict Stress curbs your ability to resolve the conflict by restricting your ability to:
- Listen actively to what is being said
- Accurately read body language and other non-verbal cues and signals
- Awareness of your emotions and the other person
- Communicate your needs clearly
- Be in touch with your deep-rooted emotions

Emotional Awareness

Emotional Awareness is vital to understanding yourself and others. If you lack emotional awareness, it would be difficult for you to communicate effectively and resolve conflicts. You may think that you know yourself well enough yet strong emotions like anger, fear, and sadness can always arise anytime. Your ability to handle conflicts will depend on how you are connected to these emotions. If you are afraid to face strong emotions and prefer to find solutions that are strictly rational, then your ability to resolve differences will be somehow limited.

Being conscious of your moment-to-moment emotional experience (emotional awareness) and the ability to appropriately handle your emotions is the basis of a communication process that can resolve issues and conflicts which is why emotional awareness is the major ingredient in resolving conflict.

Benefits of Being Emotionally Aware
- Can relate more to others
- Understand more of yourself

- Stay motivated in spite of a rising conflict
- Can communicate effectively and clearly
- Can prove to be interesting to others
- Can influence other people

Section 5

A Few Other Quickies

CHAPTER 27:

Social Media

How do you answer negative comments or destructive criticisms on your social networking site (SNS) accounts? Do you just ignore it? Do you argue or apologize?

Effectively Responding to Negative Comments on Social Media

Depending on the nature of comments and the situation at hand, your response will be affected by those. Its context will be something that only you will understand, though.

Replying to Criticism

It is only right to respond to criticism since it is inevitable nowadays, especially if you're the type that surfs social media daily. Nowadays, word of mouth means so much compared to before so one harsh comment or criticism could probably spread around the world in an instant.

If you happen to own an institution and someone criticizes it, it is only natural and important to respond to it, though constructively. Aside from being good customer service, it will reassure anyone who happens to stumble on it that you care and you're actively trying to resolve negative situations and setbacks as much as possible. In addition to that, not replying to criticisms also enforces the critique's statement, as if considering that there is nothing wrong with what they say.

Depending on the situation, you can use various options when replying to criticisms. You can either reply privately, publicly, seriously or even use some humor.

Private vs. Public

Replying privately doesn't mean that you need to talk to the critique face-to-face; it means that you can just start conversations between you two via direct messages rather than public posts. This is an effective way to use against abusive ones or for matters that need some kind of censorship. To do this, send a public reply firsthand, stating that you're sorry for giving them inconvenience and that you've sent them a private message, encourage them to resolve the matter privately.

For less irate people and smaller issues, on the other hand, leaving a public reply is a good way to show that you're helpful. If a situation looks like it can be easily resolved and won't escalate in any way, replying publicly is also a good way to promote or advertise your customer service or press relations skills.

The only major event or occasion that calls for a public reply is none other than criticisms based on baseless rumors or unfounded allegations against you or your institution. Keep in mind that you must not leave those comments without you having something to say. In these situations, you can either make a press release or offer rebuttal against their allegations and kindly ask if they want to settle matters privately. Use those depending on your judgment of the present situation.

Humorous vs. Serious

Humor can be used to show the lighter side of your personality or institution. Keep in mind, however, that it is only effective and appropriate in some situations and you need to make sure that the critiques receiving the humor will absorb it well. By analyzing the tone of voice in the comments or statements, you can decide for yourself if the person might respond to humor or it's the kind of comment that your audience will appreciate or like a humorous comment.

If the person is on the serious side, stick on replying to serious comments. Make sure, though, that your comment is never abusive even if the critique is. Keep in mind that responding aggressively or emotionally will make you or your institution look petty or childish, which will bring more harm than good to you.

Deleting Criticisms or Comments

Do not delete negative comments ever. Aside from the fact that doing this will not make the person go away, it will rather encourage them to post more negative comments. Keep in mind that negative social media users are not something you can just erase unless you're the owner of that website.

Some guides recommend deleting comments after the issue or matter has been resolved. However, there is no real harm in leaving them intact even after solving it to show that you're actively rectifying the issues and problems on your way.

Taking a Moral Stance

Certain people and institutions follow a code of conduct or principles of some kind in their society so they ought to defend those whenever someone criticizes them.

Being the kind of person or an institution willing to take a stance is a good thing for potential applicants to see. It is also good to see them participate in various discussions and debates for their improvement. Taking a moral stance may split your audience but it will leave you with better and stronger supporters compared to before. It is worthwhile to make a set of guidelines as well as a code of conduct to present a common public image.

Not Every Criticism or Comment Will be Tagged to You

Despite having the tagging feature, not all social media site users are using this all the time. Needless to say, they would leave their comments or criticisms either on their post, private messages and much more without tagging your page's handle in it.

Therefore, it will be good practice for you to check searches or public posts and respond to feedback accordingly, even if it is not directed towards you. With positive comments, you can interact with your customers and build up a much better image. On the other hand, you can also respond to negative feedback and tell the people that you're willing to actively seek effective solutions.

Always keep in mind that social media is a two-way form of communication, hence involving a speaker and listener and not just a promotional or advertising outlet. To become successful, make sure that you're always a part of that communication.

CHAPTER 28:

Random Encounters With Strangers

Generally, people connect with strangers and acquaintances on a functional level - not personal. This means they interact with them only concerning accomplishing a particular function.

For instance, you go shopping. You interact with the sales representative only with regards to the item you are buying. Once you're done buying it, you parted ways without establishing a relationship. You are not even friends and not unless you see them many times and interact many times to get familiar with each other, then they can become an acquaintance.

Connecting with strangers can happen on a personal level. When you don't have any function operating between the two of you, you may connect on a personal level. People with developed social skills find it easy to connect even with a stranger they just happen to meet on the road.

Randomly meeting strangers is a necessary part of your life. Every day, in the course of our work, we are exposed to meeting strangers, either on the road or anywhere else. If you are in business, your primary goal is to be introduced to as many strangers as you can meet and transform into clients. Even in a more relaxed social setting, meeting strangers and turning them into acquaintances are a great way to establish business relationships.

For someone who is an extrovert, meeting strangers can be fun and exciting but for most of us, we usually feel a little anxious as we try making our first impression. Who doesn't want to be well liked at by others especially those who had caught your interest?

Fortunately, we have listed here some tricks to impress strangers you are meeting.

Give Out a Genuine Smile

It's important to give out your genuine smile. It means you appreciated the work of fate guiding you on the same path. A friendly smile can warm the heart and makes one more approachable. It surely sets a positive tone for interaction and exhibits your warm and friendly nature. Moreover, science states that the simple act of smiling tricks the brain that it sends chemicals that make you feel happy. With this, you can start engaging in a positive conversation making the two of you likable at both ends.

Be Comfortable

Once you feel uncomfortable with the introduction, sure enough, the other fellow will feel it. So make sure that you are comfortable before going to meet anyone who will be introduced to you for the first time. If you have any worries, leave them all behind. You can't fake your body language or any cues your body will be sending, so make your best to be comfortable with the interaction.

For added comfort, you may use the person's name a few times. People love to hear their name called so try using it in the conversation in a natural way so the other person can feel connected and warm towards you. However, avoid using the wrong name to avoid putting yourself in an embarrassing position. Committing this crime is serious enough for you to forgo any hope of being well liked by the other party.

Have an Open Body Language

Body language is very important because actions speak louder than words. The body signals and non-verbal cues you exhibit without being aware of them talk tons and can guide the person of liking or disliking you. Also, make sure that your body languages, gestures, posture, and facial expressions are in sync with your words. Any discrepancy is sure to put you in a dilemma.

As much as possible, keep your body language open – that is, don't cross your legs, fingers, or fold your arms as it signifies dislike towards the other person. Also keep your hands out of your pocket and the direction of your toes and torso must be towards the door. This can mean that you want to get away from there.

You must be aware of the different body language signs as the other person tends to mimic your body language.

Remember that Interaction is a Two-Way Communication

Don't get too excited trying to impress the other party lest you'll end up manipulating the conversation. Apply what you have learned from previous chapters regarding communication so you won't end up boring the other person. Make sure to keep the conversation going in a direction that interests you both. Sincerely pay attention to what is being said and ask question to show that you are actively listening.

Be Yourself

Try not to impress the other and just be your natural self so you won't appear to be a fake. Remember that for them you are likewise a stranger so don't try overthinking and instead focus on things where you can have control such as the tone and direction of your conversation. You will see, matters will take care of it.

Section 6

Mindset

CHAPTER 29:

Using Habits to Change Your Mindset

Your mindset is one powerful asset you have that can either work for you or against you at any given moment. Your mindset is the key to open up opportunities you need to make a radical change in your life.

Nonetheless, not everyone realizes that when it comes to achieving their highest goal in life, it's not an action that they're missing but the incredible power that lies in their thinking, beliefs - mindset habits that can make or break their goals.

To breakthrough in your outer worlds, you have to begin within yourself. Some habits can help form a mindset that leans towards positivity and keep you away from negative energies.

Before we deal with this, let us first try to define what a habit is.

Habits are automated behaviors and rituals we perform every day. Unlike other activities and tasks we are doing and which our brain needed storage to think of – tasks like preparing coffee in the morning, taking a bath, brushing your teeth, and getting dressed are usual routines. We do all these tasks daily without thinking about them as they are already programmed in our system.

These unconscious habits free up storage for our brain to give way to more complex tasks like problem-solving and decision-making. We all have habits that are activated each day and these habits are classified into three categories.

In the first category are habits that we simply ignore or neglect because they have been with as for too long and had been incorporated into our lives. Examples of these habits are taking a bath, brushing our teeth, using utensils when eating, and putting on our slippers as soon as we arrived home from work.

In the second category, we have habits that we work hard on to establish such as doing regular exercise, reading books, eating a healthy diet, and getting enough quality sleep.

It is in the third category where habits considered bad for us belong. Habits like overspending, impulsive buying, procrastinating, and bad vices like gambling, smoking, drug addiction, and watching pornography are examples of bad habits.

According to researchers of Duke University, more than forty percent of what we are doing aren't determined by our choices but by habits. Therefore, this study suggests that we can still make some changes in our life simply by getting rid of these bad habits and creating good ones. And once we get used to these good habits, they can be retained in our brain and can be the basis of our automated good deeds.

Once good habits become embedded in our mindset, we can expect them to be a good foundation for our values and virtues which can be evident through the words we say and things we do.

Having good habits along with a great mindset will help you in your effort to develop effective social skills.

CHAPTER 30:

Why Journaling is so Important?

Some thoughts keep on lingering and feelings associated with these thoughts keep on building up. You either keep them or expressed the. You may be able to repress emotions but not for long. Repressed emotions always find a way to get out sometimes in ways we never expect. It could be through depression or any form of behavior disorder.

Journaling allows you to express yourself – a chance to say what you want to say to let your thoughts out. As you write down to express your thoughts, it allows your pent-up emotions to gradually subside until everything that was previously locked up inside you is turned into memories without vicious emotions attached to them.

Some people find it hard to put everything in a journal while others find it easy. Whether you have the talent to express yourself in journaling or not, journaling is a skill that one can learn and master with practice.

Free Journaling

Journaling starts with scribbling – writing everything that comes into your mind without filtering. You need not be concerned with committing any error – either in grammar or content. You just allow your hand to sync in with your thoughts and emotions. Just let the words flow and don't stop it. Starting can be difficult but once you have started, and your system was able to pick up the rhythm as in the melody of the song, the flow will be smoother. You may be surprised to see what comes up but just continue.

As you are writing down things in your journal, you can distance yourself from your thoughts. You can observe them without really getting attached. It's like meditation where you observe things from a distance without judgment or involvement. Because of this, you can feel your mind and your heart getting more relaxed as you go on.

You may also be surprised to find out some revelations while journaling – things you haven't thought of before but they suddenly leaped out of your mind to make you realize things you failed to realize before.

Daily Recounting

Aside from free journaling, you may also try recording your thoughts especially when you wake up in the morning. This helps you to be more transparent with yourself regarding your daily thoughts and feelings and will ultimately lead to enhancing self-awareness.

The principle of behaviorism – which is to reinforce a certain behavior through a reward system, can be incorporated in journaling by taking data about yourself and analyzing it.

To illustrate, if you are a writer, you may say that you are more productive when you have quality sleep. To test it, you may keep track of how long you sleep each day, how do you feel when you wake up – do you feel energetic or is the feeling like you haven't slept at all? How many numbers of words were you able to produce during a specific day? Be sure to write everything in your journal so it will be easy for you to review everything and make your analysis.

Creative Writing

You may incorporate journaling into your life through creative writing – writing poems and fiction stories. Because fiction is written in a freer style, they are a great way to express your thoughts and emotions through writing. You may read them aloud after writing to give yourself more freedom to express.

Journaling is an art although it can likewise be a form of science. Either way, journaling is important in communication development which is an integral part of developing social skills.

CHAPTER 31:

Improving Your Self-Esteem and Worth

Your sense of self-worth affects all areas of your life including your career, business, and relationships. Even your physical and mental health is not spared from the impact of having low esteem. But what formed your views of yourself and abilities are your experience – how people treated you – and the assessment you have made of your life and choices.

In one time or another, we all experience bouts of self-doubt. But if low esteem is hampering your performance, here are ways to build confidence and boost your self-esteem. Luckily, you have control over yourself and thus have a fair amount of control in increasing your level of self-worth. You can make some changes to challenge your body and mind. One thing you can do is to transform your negative thinking into positive ones. Building up encouraging thoughts about yourself can be a good starting point.

Get Away From Negative Thinking

Identify what triggers your negative thinking. To embrace positive thinking, you need to determine the things that promote negative thinking. There could be some situations that you can't change but somehow you can have control over your responses to these situations. Pay attention to things that make you feel anxious or sad.

Develop self-awareness. Every day, we indulge in self-talk – an ongoing dialogue that's happening in our minds. This self-talk takes notice of yourself and of what's happening around you. Take time to listen to yourself and evaluate if this thinking is based on reality or leaning towards irrationality. Does it tend to think of the worst?

Challenge your thinking. Are you always jumping to conclusions or downplaying your positive traits? If you do, then add some positive thinking to your self-talk. You need to exercise your brain to focus on the positive and avoid judging yourself. Once you make some mistakes, forgive yourself and learn to reward yourself when you accomplish something.

Take an Inventory

When you feel unsure of your self-esteem level, take an inventory of your traits and qualities. If you find yourself listing more weaknesses than strengths, it is a sign that you are quite hard on yourself. Focus more on your abilities, talents, and passion and avoid comparing yourself with others.

Remember that each of us is created to be unique. You only have to discover more of yourself each day and don't assume that you know everything about yourself.

Acknowledge Yourself

People with low self-esteem often neglect their achievements dismissing their success to luck or chance. Rather than seeing what they have achieved so far, they focus on their weaknesses and not being perfect. On the other hand, people with high self-esteem take time to be grateful and recognize their accomplishments. They are grateful when people praise them and do not dismiss this recognition. This does not imply arrogance but they have faith in themselves and their abilities.

Stop Comparing Yourself to Others

When you are always comparing yourself with someone, you are sure to see more of your weaknesses than your strengths. You'll always find someone who has better qualities than you in all aspects of your life that you will always find fault with yourself.

If you have this tendency, social media can't help you. Researchers prove that people who frequently check on social media are likely to suffer from low self-esteem. Remember that those frequently posting on social media only share the best in their life and you will never know if their weaknesses are worse than yours.

Each of us has our weaknesses and strength and when you are improving what you felt is not your strength, then you are indeed making progress.

Practice Self-Care

When you are taking care of your health, it means you are valuing yourself. Listen to your body and it will surely tell you what it needs. Living a healthy lifestyle can also increase positive thinking and improve your mood while improving your perspectives.

When you are spending more time with people who care for you, you may find it easy to care for yourself. Remember that developing a healthy lifestyle and thinking positively aren't going to give you an overnight result, but practice makes it perfect. The more that you're going to challenge your thoughts, the more that you are going to develop confidence in yourself and your abilities and as s you begin to realize you're not as weak as you think you are, you'll be looking forward to the future.

CHAPTER 32:

How to Overcome Negative Thoughts

Have you ever tried playing with building blocks when you were yet a kid? It was fun building up until they all came crashing down. Negative thinking also has the same crashing down effect in your life, career or business. Unlike the building block game, negative thinking is no laughing matter.

Thinking negatively can hinder the brain's ability to deal with complex and complicated tasks and preventing you from efficiently processing information and think clearly. Being not enough, the chronic stress resulting from negativity likewise affects the body physically resulting in illness and emotional dysfunction.

Most often, we all have negative thought patterns which we often defend by proclaiming ourselves as realists. A realist is someone who faces a situation and is prepared to deal with it accordingly. Being a realist, you can't expect constant problems and compounding them by dwelling your thoughts on them, and this can only lead to a much worse situation, but a realist will think through the challenge to find a reasonable solution.

- Are you the type of person who calmly faces every challenge and considers every possible outcome while moving smoothly through the challenge?
- Are you anticipating controversy and issues in every turn?

If you belong to the second choice, here are simple steps to consider adopting a positive mindset.

Early to Bed and Early to Rise

When you sleep early and gain enough quality sleep, you will find yourself waking up early with a smile on your lips.

You probably know firsthand that sleep affects mood. When your normal sleeping is disrupted you may be more irritable, short-tempered, and vulnerable to stress when you wake up in the morning.

When you have enough quality sleep the night before, your mood is normalized and tends to lean on the cheery side.

Studies revealed that depriving yourself of sleep even partially can have a significant effect on your mood. According to researchers of the University of Pennsylvania, participants who were slept for only 4.5 hours at night for a week came out more stressed, sad, angry, and mentally exhausted. However, when they were able to resume their normal sleep, there was a dramatic improvement in their moods.

Not only does sleep affect a person's mood but it can be vice versa. When there is anxiety which increases arousal and agitation, an individual may find it hard to sleep. So those who are constantly stressed or when they have abnormally exaggerated responses to stress, they tend to face sleeping issues.

Recognize and Step Back From Negative Thoughts

We can't help thinking of negative things. However, the problem comes in when we believe in our negative thoughts and let them affect us.

It's normal to have negative thoughts as it is part of our everyday life. Our brain is wired to be constantly on the lookout for dangers and problems which is why our mind is prone to negative thoughts. But indulging in them and allowing them to linger is what unsettle us, so it's best that you drive them away as soon as you recognized them. Once you are no longer entangled in negative thoughts, they instantly lose their power to generate unpleasant emotions for you.

Control Your Inner Critic

Do you have a harsh inner critic? Are you familiar with those nagging thoughts that tell you aren't good enough?

We have this divided personality in us. One part can be self-possessed and goal-directed while the other one can be self-denying, self-critical, and at times can be self-destructive. The second one is our inner critic which perpetuates a negative-thinking process.

Our inner voice which is the inner critic is formed out of our painful experiences in life especially during our childhood. As we grow up and experience hurtful and bad attitudes towards us, we unconsciously adopt and consolidate this pattern of destructive thoughts towards ourselves and even to others. If we cannot identify and separate this inner critic, we allow it to impact our behavior and redirect our lives from where it should be. With this, it can sabotage our relationships, dreams, and life.

CHAPTER 33:

The Importance of CBT

For people who have poor social skills, the CBT approach is important to skills crucial to socialize with others. Underlying poor social ability is a behavioral issue that needs to be identified and resolved before you can go further in improving your social skills. At this point, Cognitive Behavioral Therapy is important.

Cognitive Behavioral Therapy (CBT) is a talk therapy that takes a practical approach to problem-solving. It aims to change thinking and behavioral patterns that cause difficulties to individuals with behavioral issues to change how they feel.

CBT is used to help treat a wide range of issues including sleeping difficulties, relationship issues, drug and alcohol dependence, depression, trauma, and anxiety. CBT is geared towards changing people's behaviors and attitudes by focusing on beliefs, thoughts, and images – how these relate to individual behavior as a way of dealing with issues on emotions.

An important advantage of this talk therapy is that it is short-term, usually 5-10 months for most emotional issues. In each session, the patient and therapist collaborate to understand existing issues and develop new strategies to resolve them.

Cognitive-behavioral therapy is a combined approach using psychotherapy and behavioral therapy. While psychotherapy emphasizes the importance of how we define things and how thinking patterns start during childhood, behavioral therapy pays close attention to the close relationship between our thoughts, behavior, and issues.

CBT is personalized and customized to a patient's specific needs and personality.

CBT provides a simple approach to understanding challenging issues and problematic responses to them while emphasizing three major components:

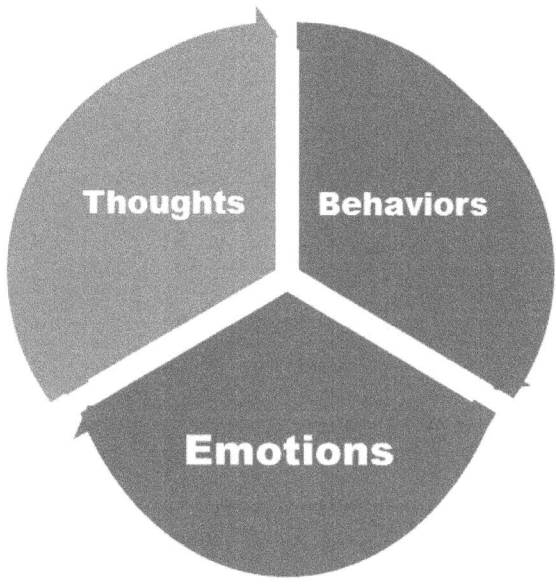

By breaking down difficult emotions, it would be easier to determine where and how to intervene to resolve a behavioral issue.

When a particular negative thought seems to result in a chain reaction of negative emotions and behavior, it is, therefore, logical to get back to the negative thought and reexamine it. If it is a behavioral pattern that is responsible, it is, therefore, more likely that a new behavior response to the issue can help resolve it.

Most often, these three components intertwine throughout the difficult stage. CBT is designed to intervene in all these three components at the same time. So in a case where uncontrollable worry is the issue, through CBT exercises, a therapist can help the patient identify more effective and grounded thoughts to lessen the feeling of anxiety.

Conclusion

Who would not want to be a social butterfly?

We all want to be like social butterflies – people who are free to fly from one place to another and always the center of attraction anywhere they go and yet aren't getting anxious or fearful of being humiliated in public.

It feels good to know that you have the confidence to deal with people from all walks of life and be able to relate to them and establish long-term connections.

Connecting with people is vital to our progress in all aspects of our lives. It's not only connecting with them but also establishing healthy relationships with them that can help us have a happy and successful life ahead.

However, being a social butterfly means that you have to fight your inner fear, face challenges, and understand yourself as you understand others.

Being a social butterfly means, you can manipulate conversations for a good reason.

As a social butterfly, you have to see the bright side of life and be the light to others.

Reading this book had prepared you to live with complete freedom like a social butterfly – FREEDOM FROM SOCIAL ANXIETY, FEAR, SHYNESS, and TRAUMAS resulting from past experiences.

This book has provided you with the basic and significant information you need to improve your social skills. As you complete your reading, we expect you to live all those things behind. They are no longer a part of who you are. YOU are now who you want to be and there's no place for negative things, people, or thoughts in your life.

You can now live freely because you choose to embrace freedom from your past. But what you have learned from this book is not enough if you won't apply it in your life. After reading, GO OUT of your nutshell and interact with people. Show them the real you – the REAL SOCIAL BUTTERFLY!

Wrapping It Up

Therefore, if you feel awkward whenever you go to social events or feel somewhat shy to talk with anyone, this could impact not only your life but a career as well. Keep in mind, however, that such behavior can be changed over time by following these strategies:

Be Sociable

Anxiety is the main reason why some people don't like to socialize with others. However, you need to be sociable to change this behavior, even if you don't feel like doing it.

Take the first step in exchanging small talk with people even if you feel nervous at first. Eventually, things will get easier as you improve your social skills.

Start Small

At first, it is expected that people having anxiety issues are finding it difficult to approach others, much more talk to them. In this case, you can start small by making it a habit of saying "Thank you" to the salesclerk whenever you buy things inside a grocery until you grow more comfortable or confident with the person.

Hold the Conversation

Maintaining the conversation is one way of putting away other's attention towards you while allowing the exchange of words on both sides. To do this, ask open questions that are not just answerable by mere yes or no but will require explanations as well.

Encourage People to Participate

Most people like to tell stories about themselves, such as stories involving their career, hobbies or achievements. If you meet such kind of people, encourage them to do so. Keep in mind, though, that you should start asking questions about their work or hobby first. Asking people about their family during your first-ever conversation could be taken as rude. And if you're asking something about their family, make sure to stick to basics such as the number of siblings, their gender ratio, age, etc.

Establish Personal Goals

Whether big or small, short-term or long-term, creating or establishing personal goals when it comes to your social life is a must. This will not only give you a particular target; it will also help you focus on matters more easily.

Give Away Generous, Not Exaggerated Compliments

Compliments make people raise their self-esteem aside from the fact that it will also give them a reason to trust and respect you. However, keep in mind that you should only give compliments that are related to their achievement.

On the other hand, giving them exaggerated compliments will make them think that you're mocking them.

Read References About Developing Social Skills

Whether in the form of paper or e-books, there are many references (mostly self-help books) about how to develop one's social skills so reading one of them isn't a bad idea at all. Since books are written according to the experiences of other people, you can also take those tips as advice.

Keep in mind, though, that reading books alone will not make you an expert overnight. In other words, you should practice whatever you read.

Exercise Good Manners and Right Conduct

Rude behavior is a bane in one's social life. If you want other people to approach and talk to you, you should exercise good manners wherever you are at all times. Be polite at all times.

Keep Track of Your Body Language

There's an old saying about actions being able to speak louder than words. When applied to social life, it can be said that people aren't persuaded or swayed by your mere words alone. The truth is, most of them pay more attention to your actions displayed during the conversation.

Keeping track here means that you should stay relaxed, give appropriate eye contact and be open whenever you talk to someone. Exercise polite gestures as well.

Join a Social Skills Group

Keep in mind that you are not alone. To make things clear, others suffer from social anxiety just like you. So for you to improve your social skills, joining a particular group is recommended. In such a group, you can practice and improve your social skills with people like you. That way, all of you will improve.

Be Updated With News and Current Trends

When it comes to improving your social skills, being updated with current events such as the new basketball league champions or latest fashion trends is a must. Depending on people's interests, being able to know worthwhile and informative news or anything interesting is also helpful. Keep in mind, however, that unless you're talking with a political analyst, talks regarding politics should be avoided as much as possible.

Think Positive

No one wants to be with negative or toxic people. In other words, staying on the negative side because of your anxiety issues is no good. Instead, assert positive things such as:

- I can do it!
- I will get to know new friends
- Life is an exciting adventure!

Take a deep breath and don't forget to smile as much as possible. That way, you will also attract positivity to yourself.

www.ingramcontent.com/pod-product-compliance
Lightning Source LLC
Chambersburg PA
CBHW072016110526
44592CB00012B/1334